Taffinder and Julia
Dunn Pulleine

Taffinder and Julia Dunn Pulleine

The Pulleine Family: From

Yorkshire, England, to America

A Story about a Couple's Life and Their Descendants

Compiled by:

Imogene H. Pulleine

iUniverse, Inc.
Bloomington

Taffinder and Julia Dunn Pulleine
The Pulleine Family: From Yorkshire, England, to America

iUniverse books may be ordered through booksellers or by contacting:

iUniverse
1663 Liberty Drive
Bloomington, IN 47403
www.iuniverse.com
1-800-Authors (1-800-288-4677)

ISBN: 978-1-4759-2938-6 (sc)
ISBN: 978-1-4759-2940-9 (hc)
ISBN: 978-1-4759-2939-3 (ebk)

Library of Congress Control Number: 2012909685

Printed in the United States of America

iUniverse rev. date: 06/30/2012

Contents

Acknowledgements

My heartfelt thanks go to Bethany Salinas of La Porte, Texas, who has been my assistant since November of 2011. In the beginning Bethany was employed by me to file a huge scatter of genealogy research proofs and separate our personal receipts and those of an estate John was acting as administrator for one of his sisters. It was soon obvious that she had a terrific memory as well as skills such as speedy computer data input.

As the weeks went by, Bethany completed a college semester at University of St. Thomas in Houston, Texas and my office space began to seem a bit larger as Bethany diligently filed and I attempted to maintain all the progress.

My chance meeting with this marvelous young person was due to the reference from a long time acquaintance and friend, Gloria Rinche, of La Porte, Texas also. I met Gloria when her children were toddlers and she was always such a happy person. She is a lovely grandmother now and seems even happier at this stage of her life. Thank you, Gloria.

On New Year's Day, 2012, I made a resolution to publish another book about our family. Normally I do not resolve to do something but I usually have a couple of goals to attain and they keep me in a very active senior citizen mode. Candace "Candy" Pulleine has nudged me to write about the ancestors stories. There are grand and great-grands that decreed the need for me to write about their Pulleine family. All of these and a couple of others are avid readers and I hope they enjoy this, if it is ultimately published.

Oh, I might not have disclosed the variance in Bethany's and my age. Bethany is a bright young eighteen year old and I celebrated my eighty-eighth birthday in December of 2011 and am very happy not to be experiencing dementia.

When I informed Bethany of my decision to publish a compilation her comment was "O.K., I am in for the long haul." She has worked with me to compile a book from many short narrative files I had stored on my computer and adding more information from our discussions about the family history and story that was being combined.

My family and friends are totally aware of how verbose I am and consequently Bethany has heard some of the tales I tell more than once.

I also want to acknowledge the diligent research of Patricia Pulleine Douglass, Earle Frost, and Jane Frost Empie. Patricia Douglass, through correspondence with Dunn cousins and trips to Yorkshire and other UK travel and research, was one of the family genealogy researchers who helped to piece together the vast amount of knowledge regarding the family. Jane Frost Empie also contributed information from some interviews she had with cousins. Earle Frost was also a genealogist for the family.

During the past couple of years I have been virtually housebound and there are a couple of other supportive people. Karin McMahan, who has worked in the house a couple of days a month for the past thirty-three years keeps the dust down and, Jose Juan Paredes, who has been with us for about three years and now not only mows but keeps the seasonal gardening changes current. As a friend of mine used to say, "One woman can't do it all."

And, to my loving husband, who is not asking questions about progress but is taking care of all his usual activities for our life style maintenance which includes grocery shopping, cooking, post office mail, banking and doing the necessary washing. He is just totally supportive and once in a while says, "I love you."

Taffinder & Julia

William Taffinder Pulleine was born in Yorkshire, England, on January 8, 1843, and died at Marysville, Kansas, on September 30, 1911. His family's home in England was Drax Hall at Drax, near Selby. Taffinder's father was William Pulleine of Newlands, Selby, born 1808, died 1892, and his mother was Mary Twigg Pulleine. They were the parents of four children. The family chart is from William Pulleyne of Dunkeswick who died in 1589 down to 1915 reference is made to "the Pulleyne's of Yorkshire."[1]

---

[1] "The Pulleynes of Yorkshire" was written by Catherine Pullein, published Leeds, England, in 1915.

Julia Dunn was born July 10, 1843, baptized August 23, 1843, at Patrington as Juliana but apparently registered as Julia, the name she was known by in the U.S.A. Her family's home was in Eastfield, Patrington, Yorkshire originally containing twenty-one bedrooms[2]. It was rebuilt in 1845 and is still a rather nice looking square brick structure as it appears in a picture which Earle W. Frost[3] has.

Through the years Eastfield was left to the unmarried daughters of the family until it was eventually sold. Julia's father was Isaac Dunn who was born in 1802 and died in 1881. Her mother, Mary Jane Raines Dunn of Burton-Pidsea in East Riding, Yorkshire, was born in 1808 and died in 1881. They were the parents of eighteen known children.

William Taffinder Pulleine and Juliana "Julia" Dunn were married March 31, 1870. They sailed for New York that same day. Their first destination, after arriving in New York City, was Virginia. Then, early in 1871 they moved to Marshall County, Kansas, and bought a farm eight miles east of Marysville, near Home City. The Pulleines and Dunns had been well to do families of Yorkshire. As children and young people in England, William Taffinder and Julia were accustomed to living in a beautiful home with all the pleasures and leisure of that time.

They built a farm in Home City in the spring of 1871. Though they saw troubling times, they worked together and made a life for themselves in Kansas.

---

[2] Photograph of the house is seen on the next page.

[3] Earle W. Frost is the author of "The Yorkshire Pulleine_Dunn Family in the U.S.A. and Their English Ancestry." It was published only for the family and did not have a copyright.

This is a copy of a photography of a painting (probably circa. 1860-70) of five daughters and one son of Isaac and Mary Jane Raines Dunn.

Old receipt reads: May 3, 1836

Rec'd of Mr. Isaac Dunn the sum of four hundred and twenty one pounds 8 shillings for building and completing a new house in Eastfield, Patterington. Sam L. Marshall

The Dunn's were married in 1824 and had eighteen children who grew to adulthood. The oldest child was born when Mary Jane was seventeen and the youngest when she was forty-four. The six oldest children were born at Ottringham Marsh.

The daughters in the painting are probably: Jemima, Catherine, Julia, Mabel and Susan. Isaac and James are the two boys seen in the picture "The Cricket Players" owned by R.M. Dunn.

Name:	**Isaac Dunn**
Age:	49
Estimated Birth Year:	Abt 1802
Relation:	Head
Spouse's Name:	Mary I Dunn
Gender:	M *(Male)*
Where born:	Burton Pidsea,
Civil Parish:	Yorkshire, England
County/ Island:	Patrington
Country:	Yorkshire
Registration District:	England
Sun-registration District:	Patrington
ED, institution, or vessel:	Patrington
Household Schedule #	10b
Piece:	239
Folio:	2364
Page Number:	176
Household Members:	60

This is an index to individuals enumerated in the 1851and 1861 Census for England. The census contains detailed information on each individual who spent the night in each household including name, relationship to the head of the family, marital status, age at last birthday, gender, the dwelling and property was collected. The Dunn's census is from 1851 and The Pulleine's census is from 1861.

Name	Age
Isaac Dunn	49
Mary I Dunn	42
Mary J Dunn	24
Francis Dunn	20
Maria Dunn	19
Anne Dunn	17
Elmor Dunn	16
Honora Dunn	13
Lucy Dunn	11
Jemima Dunn	9
Catherine Dunn	8
Julia Dunn	7
William Dunn	6
Clifford Dunn	5
Mabel Dunn	2
Ronald Dunn	1
	Mo
George Hesk	22
William Kemp	18
Charles Castle	16
Thomas Masterman	44
Ann Cranford	24
Hannah Nichelson	20
Mary J Fox	21

Name:	**William T Pulleine**
Age:	18
Birth Year:	Abt 1843
Relation:	Son
Father's Name:	William
Gender:	M *(Male)*
Where born:	Newland, Yorkshire, England
Civil Parish:	Newland
County/ Island:	Yorkshire
Country:	England
Registration District:	Selby
Sun-registration District:	Carlton
ED, institution, or vessel:	4
Household Schedule #	1
Household Members:	Name Age

Name	Age
William Pulleine	50
William T Pulleine	18
Edward Pulleine	16
Jane Barker	29
Elizabeth Lawson	21

MARY JANE DUNN'S DIARY NOTES

Mary Jane, Julia Dunn's mother, wrote in her diary around the time Julia and Taffinder were courting each other up to the time they were married and living life on their own.

[4]Referring to the diaries of Mary Jane Dunn, three separate books from August, 1864, to April, 1877, the following entries are most interesting:

---

[4]   The diary entries were put together by Earle W. Frost. When Earle compiled the publication that he distributed among family members he did not copyright it. He made this statement on his first edition 1974: "*Desiring to permit and secure the greatest possible dissemination of the information in this genealogy of the Pulleine_Dunn family, no copyright has been obtained. Any part or all may be used and reproduced without permission from the publisher so that*

1868 Nov. 29th Mr. Pulleine here also, we like him exceedingly.

1869 Jan. 31st Mr. Pulleine at Church, I like him very much.

Apr. 17th Mr. P. here to tea, pleasant as usual.

July 23rd Mr. Pulleine came to see us. I like him as well as ever. A most intelligent and pleasant companion.

Oct. 29th Mr. Pulleine came to Eastfield, pleasant and genial as ever, he looks thin, but in good spirits.

Nov. 1st At Burton with Mr. Pulleine, Julia and Maria, a pleasant evening.

1870 Feb. 20th Mr. Pulleine is here as pleasant as ever, he is a great favorite of mine.

Mar. 19th Mr. Pulleine came in the evening to stay a few days and brought Julia beautiful presents. I like him so much!

Mar. 27th All been at church with dear Julia for the last time for years, perhaps forever! May God bless and protect her is all I can pray for.

Mar. 31st Dear Julia married to Mr. Pulleine this morning, may a good God bless and prosper them! A lovely day.

July 10th Dear Julia's Birth Day. May God protect and bless her and give her many happy returns of the day.

July 14th A letter from my dearest Julia Pulleine. She writes in good spirits but likes dear old England better than America.

---

as many as possible of the descendants may have the benefit of the information herein,"

Nov. 26th   I am very anxious about my dearest Julia and pray daily for her safety. She is in Great and Good hands, Mighty to protect and Merciful to all his creatures.

1871   Jan. 18th   A letter to announce dearest Julia's safety.

Jan. 23rd   A charming letter of good news from Taff. Julia and the little babe are quite well. Julia says she has Susie's violet eyes and Grand Mama's mouth. (The baby was Hilda Muriel Zoe)

Feb. 7th   A delightful letter from America. Julia goes on well and the little one thrives.

Mar. 16th   A book has arrived from dearest Julia Pulleine for my Birthday. The dear girl never forgets her Mother in her far distant home. Oh, that she were here.

June 25th   A letter from dear Julia Pulleine. Taff has bought a farm and is building a house on the Prairie. He is having 100 cows etc. Dear Julia writes in high spirits (this would place the move to Kansas in the spring of 1871).

Nov. 11th   A letter from my dearest Julia. All well in Kansas! Julia likes housekeeping very much.

1873   Aug. 11th   A letter from dearest Julia and likeness of Guy and Hilda.

1874   Oct 12th   Dreadful news from dear Taff. Their sweet little Hilda Zoe is dead & they are very sad. She died on the 10th of Sept. I wrote by return post.

1876   Mar. 28th   A letter from dear Taff announcing safe confinement of dear Julia, of a little girl on the 3rd of March (Myrtle Pulleine Frost).

July 11th   Poor Freddy's B-Day. Yesterday was dear Julia's __ Alas! Alas! For the dear days gone by never to return.

July 31st   A letter from dear Frederic (USA) announcing that he is in bad health and unable to do much work.[5]

---

[5]   A long time major mystery finally has been solved regarding the burial place of Frederick Dunn in the U.S.A. was unknown. Thanks to the good efforts of Marjorie Louise Pulleine (Marge), the gravesite has been located. She got in touch with the Woodmere Cemetery and was advised that their records did show that Frederick Dunn was buried in a single grave, Section A, Block 176, Grave No. 7, age 38, and date of December 25, 1876, as the result of a liver complaint.

The following narrative was written by Taffinder and Julia Pulleine's youngest son, Percy Pulleine. He wrote about his parents and his home life during his youth. Percy had been a banker and a probate judge with secretaries to perform necessary typing chores but he wanted to share his parent's story so his knowledge has been transcribed from a document with many typing errors. It was decided to leave it exactly as Percy had written it, fixing no grammatical errors, in order for it to remain in his vernacular.

PERCY PULLEINE'S NARRATIVE

Around the year 1869 in Hull, Yorkshire, England William Taffinder Pulleine and Julia Dunn were married. He was from a well to do family who lived on a farm called Owsley Ferry. The bride, Julia, had a maid and was not versified in cooking, washing, ironing and sewing and was hardly fitted to take over the duties of a housewife if necessary. A neighbor who had gone to America and had written and told them of the glowing opportunities in the new land so it is easy to see why they decided to leave the old for the new. The groom had come into a comfortable sum, possibly $ 30,000. and his Uncle Samuel, who lived at Drax Hall not far away asked him not to leave and that if he didn't he would come into his possessions. The uncle being a single man and the groom being the eldest of his nephews would inherit. Drax Hall was not a castle just a nice large house with quite a large acreage.

William, the groom, could not resist the lure of the new country and gave up the easy life as an English squire. I ran across old cricket sheet years ago and among the members names was that of my father listed as Squire. His uncle Samuel died when in his nineties several years after my father, and to us children he left 500 pounds, to a cousin Drax Hall. The cousin was thrown from a horse soon after and killed and Drax Hall passed to his young widow, to several cronies he left around 30,000 pounds. This foregoing recital is just to show the background of a couple of Innocents who like millions of others were migrating to new lands.

Back to my story: On their way, it being also their wedding trip, they stopped in London and often regaled us children with tales of the sights they had seen such as London Bridge, the Cathedral, the Thames and many other sights. They told also of hearing Jenny Lind sing, how the audiences, spellbound, held their applause for awhile. Then they made the long trip across the Atlantic. They first stopped in Virginia and there my eldest brother, Guy Addison (the poet Addison was a distant relative) was born, remembered well is a picture of him on a Negro nanny's lap. In those days well to do Englishmen had little protection from sharpies and father lost quite a bit of his money, how I never knew. Eventually they arrived in Marysville, Kansas, I believe in early 1871. They stopped at the Anderson House, although it might have been the Tremont.

A Marysville old timer told me years ago that it was quite a sight to see father with his topper (his leather hat box was at least two feet high) and mother in silks and satin and brother in a velvet suit. A friend he had known in England, English Bill Lewis, lived in the northwest corner of Sec. 26 and father homesteaded an eighty in the SE corner of the same section (80 acres was all one could homestead in those days) and bought some land across the road. He had a large two story house built and the carpenters one Sunday said the house is completed and you can move in. On the following day, full of hope and pride, they moved out only to find that a tornado had completely demolished the new home. All that was found was some window panes scattered over the prairie.

So with the faith that all pioneers must have they built again, this time a one story with an attic and the walls were filled with rocks and bricks. A year or so later there came a little girl and when she was three years old became sick and they thought that she was almost well. One day mother was alone in the home with her and she looked up and said "goodbye, mother" and died. It is needless to dwell on the pain and agony of a young mother alone in the home with the lifeless body of a beloved child and the nearest person miles away.

To the North of us, some twelve miles just across into Nebraska was the Otoe Indian Reservation and mother quite often told of how when they stopped by she had to keep them out of the house as they were well supplied with vermin that always seemed glad to leave the Indian bodies. The dogs had to be kept hidden as they were considered very desirable for a meal by the Indians and the feast of the fat hogs that had died of cholera and lay bloating in the sun and soon disappeared in the Indians hungry stomachs.

Twice, in the Seventies (1870's) came the grass hoppers so thick that the Sun was hidden and how soon all vegetation was consumed. Families were left without food and no money to buy any so two or three families moved in and father and mother simply said that you couldn't let them starve. Then to the north of our home the Yankee Bill Lewis home burned. A daughter of that family told me, "Your Dad gave some money for the lumber and the other neighbors having none built the new house. Also, her mother once told her that Mrs. Pulleine had said to her 'if you will only teach me how to wash, sew and cook." Old timers realize what a tragedy to transplant a lady who had always had a maid to do things for her out onto the Kansas plains to be a pioneer mother. Father was well educated and had been sent to a boarding school at the age of six. When I saw the movie "Mr. Phipps goes to school" I realized some things I had never understood before.

Father was 5'8" with dark blue eyes and sideburns, a square face and rather wiry. Not given to praise so that if we did some things that a parent might praise we were given to understand that it was only what we should have done. He held all the township offices and people were always going to him for advice. In those early days after a long trip to town in a wagon

13

the men would imbibe too freely and the wife would have to drive home. One day a Mrs. McS in driving home and going up a hill Mr. McS rolled out of the wagon where he had laid down in the bed of the wagon and the good lady drove all the way home ignorant of what had happened. Don't laugh. That meant eight hours to where he was and back home after having already driven five hours in a jolting lumber wagon. Next morning they appeared at our home to tell father their troubles. She weighed about 250 lbs. and was all muscle. After listening to their story father said, "and what did you do Mrs McS.?" She replied, "I do this" and she swung her huge hand out across father's chest and completely bowled him over. Father had a sense of humor and always laughed about it.

In the early days in the hot summer time a death one day meant a funeral tomorrow. A neighbor, a corpulent Irishman died one hot July day and for some reason the funeral was delayed and when the time came only a few of the pall bearers were able to enter the room and carry out the body.

In the early 1880's father moved to the small town of Beattie nearby. I never knew why but presumed it was because of poor crops and dwindling money. Within two years he moved the family back to the farm. I have heard my brother say while they were off the farm there were good years for the farmers.

Then came the 80's (1880's) and we were a growing family. Mother always named thee girls after flowers and we boys had English names. Well remembered are the evening when father would start early in the morn for the mill to have wheat ground into flour. While probably 20 miles it took many hours and in the evening in the dusk we would group along the road waiting for the rumble of the wheels. In the air the night birds would zoom and scream and in the distance the howl of the coyote. With the bright stars and the soft breeze from the South all seemed so peaceful as we eagerly awaited the small sack of candy.

About this time there were four of us going one mile to District 105 (school). Then there were the neighbors as section 26 was now thickly settled, three (3) Parks families to the West along with the Martins then north Yankee Bill Lewis with English Bill and his family in the NW corner, then Beavers in the north center and Enoch Manning's right in the center. He homesteaded there but the neighbor gladly gave him a road out.

Then in the Fall of '88 in the middle of the night father awakened us children and loaded us in the lumber wagon to be driven by our oldest brother. Not even knowing what it was all about I can still remember the stars above us, the jolting wagon as we crossed the railroad. Arriving at the Manning home brother said to the lady who answered his knock, "Father says to come at once" and in a few minutes she was out and the wagon rumbled away. Those were the days when neighbors were neighbors. Time dims the memories but well remembered are our teacher's words when she announced to the school that there was a little baby girl in the Pulleine home. How we ran all the way home and mother held the little tyke for us to see. She was a beautiful child with light hair and deep blue eyes and enchanting smile. None of us ever complained when asked to rock the cradle and shoo the flies.

A few years later father bought the first registered cow to come to this county; she had a long pedigree and came from Pawnee City, Nebraska (the cow). Her name was Belva Lockwood and was quite old and was probably the reason he was able to buy her. Shortly after Belva, the second, came and the cow and calf were tethered out near the house. While watching the new calf the little sister wandered over that way and the mother cow rushed at her and just before she hooked her she stumbled and fell. Mother came scramming to the rescue and carried the little girl out of the cows reach. Saved this time but only to have a tragic (accident) and as will be told later. I, myself, had a narrow escape a few years earlier while visiting at the English Bill Leis home. Families would go on a Sunday for a visit in each others homes. That Sunday Emma Jane, a (Lewis) daughter, came home in the afternoon driving a large herd of cattle and of course I had to go have a look. A cow, with a new calf, came rushing at me and fortunately caught me between her horns. Emma Jane carried me to the house and I came to on a couch. I had no injuries.

When the families would go visiting on a Sunday it was always a great event. Many months could pass without seeing a single stranger and the visiting peddlers were always welcome and long into the night we would set listening to news. In 1888 came Barnum Circus to Marysville and into the lumber wagon were we all bundled on the straw in the bed of the wagon with father sitting high up on the seat and driving the team. When we were about a mile East of Marysville looking back over the road all you could see was nearly a solid line of lumber wagons, the only others going that way was the young blades riding by on horse back, shouting and waving their hats as they went by. Then arriving there neighbors grouped together for dinner. The children gazing open mouthed at the city sights, the sound of the blaring circus band, the parade, then at last out to the circus in the Northeast part of town. (Now covered with homes) Then all but mother went in to the big tent. I often wondered why she didn't go in and it was many a year until a conclusion was reached. It was just a short time before the little sister was born. In those days expectant mother took no chances on something that might affect the unborn child. The only things I remembered of that circus is the educated pig and Shetland ponies racing with monkeys as riders. Other amusements were the school lyceum; there would be recitations, plays and debates. Every so often would come slickers who would put on a show and sell different articles. They always had a contest to sell votes for the prettiest girl in the District. My eldest sister won one. As I look back now it wasn't good as the contestants and friends and families on each side spent money they could ill afford and left some bitterness in the District.

Then there were the spelling contest where sides were chosen and the match ended when only one was left in the line. Then one of our teachers, instead of spelling, had ciphering down. It ran like this . . . 4 x 4 minus 3 plus 7 x 2 divided by 8. Then those on each side would give the answer and the first one correct was the winner. This teacher was a Civil War vet and most remembered his ability to hit the coal bucket, feet away. He liked his chewing tobacco. Both types (of contests) were very helpful to the students. Books of those days always had a moral in all readers. One can but regret the passing of the McGuffey books. Games played, "Anti Over", "One hole cat", "Rosy round the ring", and "dropping the handkerchief".

You may have heard about the ministers and fried chicken and they are not entirely without some truth. One day in the '80's two came to our home and being forewarned we children caught the chickens and soon they were ready for the frying pan. Then, with all our elders around the table and we peeking through the door saw the chicken plates passed and passed until we thought there would be nothing left. We grew up and finally acquired a taste to the backs, gizzard, etc. and of course, when our children grew up it was a good thing (for them) for now the parents watch the children eat first.

Kirk, the farm boy who came to dinner took a whole spoonful of horseradish and father said, "Go steady, Kirk." Boy like, he replied, "I like it" and downed the whole spoonful. How those tears streamed down on his plate but he manfully stood his ground. He was not like the boy who at a dinner of many guests took a mouthful of hot food and spit it out on his plate and then said, "Some dern fool would have swallowed it."

Times were again getting rather hard, as farm crop failures and depressions come and go with exceeding regularity. Baked Jack Rabbit stuffed with sage was quite often a Sunday dish and in those days tasted mighty good. The tables did not groan with food and when father came home with a can of salmon we children would vie with one another to see who could eat the most slices of bread with his or her portion. Father was very particular to see that each got an equal share.

Father was meticulous in every thing he did. His corn rows were nearly half a mile long and perfectly straight and many a neighbor driving by stopped to admire them. One day he and four of us children were going down the corn rows, each with a hoe and seed corn, cutting the weeds and planting corn wherever a stalk did not appear. A skunk just ahead of us started down a row and father took aim with his hoe and caught the animal back of the head. Death was so sudden there wasn't even a smell. English Bill told of father shooting a deer with a rifle and killing it instantly over in District 105.

English Bill was a torment in my life. He had red whiskers and he would rub his face against mine and then tell me mine would be red. Father brought from Eng. Bill many works by the great writers. Many books had large ivory letters on the outside backs; there were desks, much jewelry, and I remember seeing hoops for skirts in the attic. Father, hearing a quotation from any of the great works, could tell from what book it came. He would have been at home on the "64 thousand" program. He offered any of us children $ 10.00 if we would read Milton's Paradise Lost" and gained. No one won it. If we could only have saved the wonderful articles they brought with them. Hardly any are left.

Mother liked to play cards, dominoes, etc. and many an evening was passed in this manner. We always had to win the hard way as our parents did not believe in letting us win as it wouldn't be good for us.[6]

As we lived up on the level land and father had bought a 5 acre track down on the Vermillion River so the wood would be cut from there for the winter fuel and I can still see him coming in with a load (of wood) on a cold day and standing over the fire while the ice melted off his whiskers

Along about this time, one evening we were along the railroad that passed through the North part of the farm gathering ties. The section boss would tell the farmers to take the ties but always in the nighttime. A meteor came from the East and I believe it lit Washington County (Kansas). It was brighter than daylight and you could feel the heat and it seemed just over our heads. This same evening a crowd of boys from Home City were out getting some melons and when the meteor went over one dropped his melon and got down on his knees and prayed.

In Home there were always several fights generally on election day. One fight to be remembered was that of Eng. Bill and Barney. an Irishman. Both were big and powerful, however their difference always ended, as they could not have any fun unless they were arguing with one another. There was the story of the time with a load of ties they were going along the road and got into one of their red hot arguments. It was a warm day and both seemed to get warmer and warmer, even took off their coats. And then, one looked behind and saw that the ties were on fire. A tie had dropped down and rubbed against the wheel. In those days there were many fights between individuals and groups. There was one between Myers W. and Lash S. that lasted a half day. There were the Irish from Beattie and Swiss

---

6   When she had a stroke in later life, her husband, Taffinder, wrote her family
     in England to say that she was able to play cards because she was right handed
     and could still shuffle cards with that hand.

from around Home, the Irish, Germans and Canadians from Southwest of town and when together generally ended in free for alls. One that came home to us was when a group from Beattie came over to Home. When my brother, 18, came out of the dance hall a man, several years older and much larger, jumped on him without any provocation and beat him badly. For many days I remember mother's cries when he came home with loss of teeth and beaten face. Father brought action but the fellow from Beattie skipped out.

One day in the early 90's the corn was laid by, very clean and now tasseling. Father said, "We will take a day off and go down to the timber claim (the 5 acres) on the way down we passed neighbors farm and there the corn was all weeds and father stopped the wagon and said, "Notice how that field looks to what ours does." Alas, no rain and the hot winds blew and our corn turned yellow and cried up. Then later the rains came and the neighbor's corn, held back by weeds, had around 25 bushels per acre. As we didn't know that would happen we had a happy afternoon and I caught my first bullhead.

At school meeting quite often many disturbances occurred. At District 10 Pete and Lem got into a fight and Pete bit off Lem's finger and Lem swore he was going to kill Pete. All summer Pete, who was with a threshing crew, practiced shooting and as he just didn't have the knack, Lem needn't have worried. Then one rainy afternoon Lem was driving a load of children from school and Pete came by on a mule and after he was about 50 feet from Lem shot him through the back of the head. Later that evening Pete's brother, Mart, stopped at our home and said, "Lem shot Pete, what shall I do?" and Father said, "Go home, Lem is now in Marysville in the Sheriff's hands." Later the neighbors, one night, formed a mob to lynch Lem and when they appeared at the jail the Sheriff gave him a gun and he fired into the crowd. In later years a fellow died and the story was that he was hit that night by Lem. Lem was given 5 years. His attorney was able to get this because Pete had married the girl and talked what he would do. He wouldn't have hurt Lem, just talking to boost his courage. Lem's reputation was very bad in many ways but he had a lot of nerve and American people quite often forget the evil because the person in question has some commendable trait. This is a story told about Lem, how he went into the town of Beattie and the Marshall there had said if he came to town he would kill him. Lem unloaded his grain out of his wagon; while replacing endgate the Marshall shot at him 6 times and Lem went on with his work of putting end gate in place, paid no attention to eh bullets hitting around him. When the shells were gone, the story goes that, the Marshall threw the gun away and started up the creek and was never seen in Beattie again.

Brother Guy went to Oklahoma to run for a farm at the opening of the Strip. He had no luck.

Hard times came again and Cox's army marched to D.C. We saw a few as they passed our farm. Then as I herded cows, I could see a mile South on the old Marysville-Nemaha roads covered wagons all day long, going West. On the wagons would be signs such as "Back home to wife, folks, and a full meal" "In God we trusted and in Kansas we busted", etc. As they went along you could get a dog or some other cherished keepsake at your own price. To know the tragedy, sorrows, and hopes of the farm people you must have been there. How, many of a time has the farmer planted his crops, fought the weeds, borrowed the money and labored long hours then the hot winds blow day after day, no rest at night. Dust, sweat and tears and in time all hopes go as the crops withered and died, but hope springs eternal with hope that there will always be a good year ahead.

And, how many times did the clouds come and it seemed that any moment from the heavens would drop cooling rain. The crops would seem to gather new life, then all faded away and the sun again cast its hot breath upon the land. Then in the small town of Home came Mary Ellen Lease with her talk of the Farmers raising more hell and less corn. Along this time came the Populist Party as the new deal. There is the story of the German boy, Jno., who when asked to go and hear the lady replied, "Nein, I think I plow die corn." Not many years later Jno. owned most of those same neighbors' farms. I expect you can find the lesson.

Father was now discouraged and I expect his money was nearly gone. He had held nearly all township offices and decided to run for Probate Judge. Mother had always been ailing as she was afflicted with rheumatism and her screams of pain was often heard. Father made his campaign over the county by driving a cart with a big sorrel horse named Charlie. He covered the whole county but lost by eight (8) votes.

Father must have always been easy for the horse dealers. There was Dick the roan, balky and when he stopped nothing you could do but wait until he decided to go. There was the story of the balky horse whose owner built a fire under him. The horse moved up and the wagon contents were burned. Charlie was a different type. When hitched and asked to go he would always back up in a circle so many times before he started straight out. In those days, remembrance of a threshing machine is one with two horses in a box elevated at one end and as they started walking they furnished the tread power to operate the separator. Then came the horsepower where about a four to six team were hitched and went around in a circle. Then on each side of the separator the loads of grain would come, then in the center would be the feeder and on each side of the band boys who cut the strings on the bundles. As it was cut the feeder reached out and put the grain into the mouth of the separator then on through to the stacker then on to the strawstick. This last was the worst job all as the stackers caught all the dust and dirt that came through with the straw.

Years ago came a story that created consternation all over the country. A reporter started it in a Wichita paper about how a feeder cautioned a band boy who accidentally cut his hand that if he did again he would throw him to the separator. It happened and the feeder did what he said. How many tears were shed over a story that was not true. Corn shelling was quite a job especially if the farm was some distance from market. There were the shovellers who all day fed the corn into the sheller then the ones who took the corn to market and as it took around 5 to 10 hours some of the haulers in order to be first would be at the shellers as early as 3 a.m. so as to get the first load. No help was hired, always neighborly help. Have watched father mow with a scythe, the steady rhythmic swing, always piling the clover or hay in a neat row, only straightening up to sharpen the scythe. Then thee woe of the farm wife, the trip to town to get the meat etc to feed 20 men, more or less, and if the threshing crew didn't get there how to save the food. No refrigeration of any kind, only the well to hold the butter and deeper the well the cooler the butter.

Father having signed too many neighbor notes now had a small grocery store on his hands. He again ran for office and this time was elected. When he passed on his assets were mostly worthless notes.

The crops grown were wheat, oats, corn, and some flax. The corn was planted by machine called the planter. Strung out was a row of wire with nobs at the distance the corn kernels should be dropped and as the planter went down the field the kernels were dropped the nobs caused the dropping. If planted you could look down the rows from any direction or if listed the furrow was made then a one row drill pulled by a horse dropped the seed corn. The first cultivation was by the Go Devil, a long box with knives a foot or so long attached to the side of the box. This machine would do down the row. If the driver did not ride the box then a weight would be placed on it. Next would come the cultivator; most of the early ones didn't have a tongue and when you turned at the end of the row quite often collapsed. However they did a good job. As the riding cultivators etc didn't come into our parts until around '95 (1895) all field work was done by walking, all day from sun up until sun down then back home to do the chores and up again at 4 a.m. Cows to be milked and fed and the horses to be curried and fed, oats from the bin and hay from the loft or stack outside. The hired man pay of that era was around $ 15. per month and keep. If here today they would think they were in paradise.

Father had several acres of orchard, peaches and apples, and they were the Genitons, Ben Davis, early harvest. Early June, Maidens Blush, Snow or Strawberry, Winesaps, Jonathan, Baldwins, and a few others. The trees would be loaded and no worms but what was worse was no market. Remembering taking into town some but none would buy and they ended as feed for the hogs. Father had quite a large field of Red Clover, the only one I can remember in the neighborhood. When the neighbor boys came what a time we had with the bumble bees. We became experts of being able to hold without getting stung until the small drop of hone was taken from the poor bee. While this seems cruel, remember sweets for the children were far between in those days. This was while cutting the clover.

Another chore in those days was getting ready for company on the summer days. Every child was given a broom and then from room to room we went shooing the flies from out of the house. The blinds were then all pulled down so as to keep the house dark. Another chore was carrying water to the fat hogs on a hot day. Another chore was carrying water to the fat hogs on a hot day. Well remembered was the day when mother and we small ones were alone and from the barn 200 feet away came the wheezing of the hogs, mother routed us out and from the well

90 feet deep was hauled the water to be carried to the suffering hogs but to no avail. A loss that could be ill afforded.

Being the youngest boy I was let down in that same well by a long rope to retrieve a bowl of butter that had slipped from its holder. It was cold down there and a long way to the top. It furnished just enough water for the house and the live stock had to be taken some distance for water. Like lots of other Kansas farms it was short of water, a serious matter.

Father was always trying different things and one year had a large watermelon patch and the crop was excellent. Then one night about 25 fellows on horse back raided it and did much damage. Our neighbor to the East, a German who still talked brokenly came over and he thought it was quite funny. Corn was just past the roasting year stage and a very fine crop. A few hours later the old fellow came running back and it was some time before father could make out what the trouble was. It seemed the boys took our melons into the middle of his corn field and let their horses feed while they ate the melons. He wanted them hung. Father winked at mother and said, "It all depends on whose ox is gored." Have heard him say if you want to know what a fellow is get him drunk and whatever he is will be plainly shown. He always kept liquor in the house for guests but drank but little. Another expression was that, unfortunately are only two ways to drink it, like a gentleman or a hog.

Our family was Episcopalians, but with no church near, we went to the M.E. church in Home where it was a pleasure to hear tunes sang with fervent ardor. John Thomas, who had charge, led the singing of the good old hymns and his voice filled the church, like Rock of Ages and nearer my God to Thee. It wasn't unusual to walk one to three miles to church and lyceum affairs and the same to go skating and always walking back in a crowd, generally talking and singing. Then in 1890 to the wedding of Polly Ann and Thomas in the big new house and there Robert John, unmarried and older than Polly Ann had to dance in a hog trough that had been brought in to the kitchen. Just a custom. Another treat was a trip to Marysville and especially we went through the yard of Banker Koester. His home was on Main Street and covered ¾ of block with a high brick wall around it. Inside (the yard) were statues of birds, animals and people and a greenhouse. I expect about the first one West of the Missouri River. He was known as the politest man in the county.

The early 90's (1890's) times for farmers were bad. Father sold the farm, was elected to the office of Probate Judge and we moved to Marysville. The farm brought $35. per acre. In 1910 it was worth $100 per acre and after WWI $200. Then in the late 30's (1930) about $35 with more improvements. Today rather think could be sold for $200 per acre. In a century Kansas farms will go up and down, all depending on the crops. Landowners in Kansas in good years will be wealthy. In depression years, poor, but if he keeps his farm free of debt he will survive, leaving a farm of course meant a farm sale and as times were hard some livestock and equipment sold very cheap, calves $6. up, cows around $30 to $40. per head and horses as low as $35. In good times cows would bring $75 and horses as high as $200. Once in awhile a good mule team would bring $500.

Marysville being the County seat, there we moved. The neighbors came with the lumber wagon and household goods were loaded, with three horses and one cow we started, and probably four hours later arrived at the new home. In those days nearly every family had one or two horses and one cow or more. During the summer months the cows would be driven to pastures quite often adjoining the town, head across the river to the pasture there, another to the North and two to the East and two to the South. These were jobs to the city boys, the pay was from twenty cents to fifty cents per month for driving the heard to and back each day and there was plenty competition for the jobs. A penny in those days was more to a child of that day than a dollar is to the child of today.

Mother was still ailing and was bed ridden most of the time with much pain. We children started to school, brother Sam and I being in the 8th grade (the highest grade in a country school) and sister Hyacinth was all placed in the same 8th grade. Hyacinth being a good student went through high school in three years so graduated ahead of myself and Sam. Sam quit high school to take a job. In those days all fun was made by the boys and girls. We bought our footballs, baseballs and uniforms (if we had one) paid our way to go to the games in other towns. If the school put on a play it was free most of the time. Most of the time was taken in class recitations, school from 9 to 12 with a few minutes recess. If caught in a misbehavior you didn't dare run home crying to your parents for you would probably get more than the teacher gave you. From the time school took up the teachers were busy all day hearing classes. The only holidays were the legal ones and there weren't many. I can't remember in our high school of around 50 any pupil wearing glasses. One boy smoked, didn't graduate and died a few years later it was said from T.B. (tuberculosis). Might have been cancer of the lungs. This was held up to all as an object lesson.

Time went on and in 1900 another tragedy entered our lives, especially Mother's. The little sister playing with another small girl where a fellow was hauling sand came too close and the sand caved in and all in sight was one small arm. The other little girl ran screaming home to mother who ran to the pit and when others arrived had the sand from around her head.[7] Father died at the age of 69, he had never been sick a day in lifetime and mother who had always been ailing died a few years later.

---

[7]   The little girl was named Trixie. Her story is continued after Percy Pulleine's Narrative.

In the early 1900's, in every small town, there were always ten single women, mostly widows to one single man of mature age. One wonders why as nearly all of the women worked harder and longer hours, large families, washing, ironing, sewing and the first one up in morning and the last to bed and always to the neighbor homes in times of sickness. Was it the out door exposure that took the men early in life? If so, what about the young females of today who go racing around in zero weather, barelegged and not much clothes? I shiver when I see one.

Never did I ever hear mother regret of coming to the new country, leaving a life of ease for one of toil, pain and sorrow. This might be closed with a true story. Having tone back to the small town of Home and there one summer day Bill, an old timer, was talking to me on the street when there came along a little ole woman hobbling along and as she passed said, "Howdy, gents". Bill turned to me and said, "Did I ever tell you about Plenty to eat/" and I said, "Shoot". Bill in early days had a threshing machine and in those days would start around the neighborhood and line up jobs, some time not getting back for a long time. He said he arrived at the old lady's home one evening to get their threshing and talking to farmer and his wife with a group of red headed freckly faced children standing around eagerly listening. Finally started to leave when Mrs. P. said stay all night, Bill. We have plenty eat and Bill said that was all the invitation needed.

But, he added, when we sat down to eat all in the world on that table was parched corn but there was plenty of it. A short time later Mrs. P., now a widow, called me and said she had sold her farm and would I come down and make out the papers. I replied that I had never done any of her business and she replied, "Your old Pappy always took care of our troubles and deals and I wish you would. So down to her home and there was the neighbor who was buying the farm. Asked if she was wise in selling she said, "It is a good price," which was correct, and the children need the money. The neighbor was an honest and reliable fellow so I wrote out the deed and placed it in front of her. Then as she slowly wrote her name I heard her saying something and I stooped a little to listen and this is what I heard. "God has been mighty good to me, mighty good to me." And as I looked at that knarled hand with crooked, swollen fingers, from hard work, the faded eyes and wrinkled skin, the white hair, stooped shoulders, the wear and tear of more than three score and ten years and there came back to me Old Bill's story, "Plenty to eat, plenty to eat." How grateful we should be that the pains and sorrows of a lifetime fade away and there is left only the pleasant memories.

Trixie

On the morning of July 24, 1900, the youngest Pulleine child, Beatrice Mabel Ivy, widely known as Trixie, had risen early to help her big brother, Percy, who was preparing to ride out to the farm of his sister, Mrs. John Frost. On that summer morning she ran down to the stable, saddled Percy's horse and brought it back to him. After waving goodbye to her brother, Percy road in the direction of the Frost farm in Walnut Township. The eleven year olds thoughts then turned to play at her favorite spot on the sandbank below her home. The towering wall of sand was a child's delight where imagination and childish hands could create a fantasy world of caves and castles.

At 5 o'clock that afternoon Trixie and her playmate, May Ruggles, were playing house in a cavernous hole in the bank were workmen had recently removed several loads of sand. The little girls were making 'lemon pies' which required white and yellow sand. May ran out of the cave to replenish their supply of white sand for their pretend baking. When she returned to the playhouse the murderous amount of sand came sliding down just as the two children met at the opening of the cave.

Failing in her rescue attempts to free Trixie from the sand, May ran up the hill crying out for Trixie's mother. Julia Pulleine raced down the hill and frantically clawed and dug at the sand entombing but by the time Trixie was extricated, she was dead.

Two days later the funeral was held at the Pulleine home. The grief of the bereft Pulleine family was shared by many who mourned the death of bright vivacious Trixie, who was the favorite of both young and old.

In memory of Trixie the family donated a baptismal font to St. Paul's Episcopal Church in Marysville, Kansas.

"*This (the poem) was written when we were in Western Kansas on the cattle ranch where the wind whispered poetry to me thru the short grass. I always wished to send it to the family but lacked the courage. 'Trix' had been one of 11 little girls at Lura Scott's 12th birthday party. Prof. Scott was my brother in law. So this tragedy occurred 38 years ago*"

-Mrs. Maggie Hartman Scriber Reneau

"The Fate of Trix."
A True Story

Two litte girls one Saturday,
Went to an old sand cave to play.
Maud (May) was ten and Trix was twelve,
But each did work and each did delve
Making mud pies? Yes, lemon pies.
Loud their daughter and loud their cries
For more white sand and more yellow sand.
Oh! Little they knew of the treacherous sand!
The glistening, gleaming yellow sand!
The creeping, crumbling fine white sand!

What fun 'twould be, cried one sweet maid,
If the sand would cave. Down she laid
The pie she had finished. Ere Maud spoke,
Back in the hill the sand bank broke;
With sudden force the sand came down;
It covered Maud's feet and held her down
But of Trix—with all her children grace,
Nothing was left to mark the place
Where she had stood, but a mound of sand.
Of treacherous, heavy, yellow sand.

Two hundred feet above, on the hill,
Stood the Mother's house. Maud stopped
On the sill,
And told as best she could, the Mother,

Then off she ran to tell another.
Quickly then the Mother started ;
Down the winding path she darted;
Running, slipping, tumbling down,
She reached the place where the sand was brown.
Heavy and fresh she could plainly see,
And there she knew her darling should be.

Ah! Pitiful task to that Mother given!
Surely the strength was lent from Heaven!
With frantic haste she dug the sand
Away, away, till she found a hand.
Soon another and then the face.
Gone, alas! All childish grace.
Gone all light and life from her eyes.
Gone! To her home with Him in the skies!

Soon others came. One with a spade.
Then the fair lifeless form was laid
Upon the sand; while from every heart
Prayers to God, for the Mother, start.
Oh, warn your children of the sand!
Every Mother in the land!
Of the glittering, glistening yellow sand!
Of the creeping, crumbling fine white sand!
Or else, someday misfortune dire,
She'll wreak upon you in her ire.

Percy & Gertrude

Gertrude Hamilton was born on a farm near Blue Rapids, at the Hamilton home, September 16, 1885. She received her education in the schools of the county and graduated from Blue Rapids high school in 1902. In the graduation ceremony she did the oration entitled Noblesse Oblige. Later she attended Kansas State Teachers' college at Emporia. She taught in Cottage Hill Township and for five years was an instructor in the Centarl grade school in Marysville.

In 1909 she was united in marriage with Percy Pulleine at the family home in Blue Rapids. They lived for a short time in Marysville but for the next twenty years they resided in Home City, where Mr. Pulleine had been in banking and the insurance business.

Mrs. Pulleine became the mother of six children, Alice, Patricia, Margaret, John William and Marjorie. The youngest is one of twins, the other, Edwin, having died within twenty-four hours of birth in 1922.

People considered Mrs. Pulleine to be a woman of remarkable gaiety and charm, combined with great sympathy and common sense and she endeared herself to many friends wherever she went. Her general health had been good up until two years before her death, when she developed a stomach disorder which necessitated an operation. Her condition was critical the last few months. Through all of her illness she was cheerful and brave and set a wonderful example of Christian fortitude.

Mrs. Percy Pulleine, a lifetime resident of Marshall County, passed away at the home of her mother, Mrs. Alice Hamilton near Blue Rapids, on a Friday afternoon, following a prolonged illness. She was aged 46 years, 10 months and 13 days.

Percy Pulleine was born on November 23, 1880 at Home, Kansas. He graduated from MHS in 1900. Following the footsteps of his father, William Taffinder Pulleine, Percy was a longtime county official, served more than 20 years as a probate judge. He was a longtime member of St. Paul's Episcopal Church and Marysville Rotary Club. In the forty years he was a member, he never missed a meeting. He was also on the draft board for World War II. In the early 1930's he had to declare bankruptcy because the loans to the farmers could not be paid due to weather conditions. It was said that Percy paid back, from his own pocket, the stockholders who didn't receive their money during the Depression. At the age of 95, he passed away at Community Memorial Hospital, where he had been a patient one week.

From time to time some business question would arise that he would consider amusing and take the time to send it to one of the monthly news magazines. The following was published in TIME on February 26, 1956, under MISCELLANY: O Promise Me: In Marysville, KS Probate Judge P. R. Pulleine received a request from an absent-minded husband. *Will you please tell me the name of the woman I married there in 1918?*

During the mid 1960's we met a new neighbor and acknowledging our last name she inquired about the name of his home town. She was from Beatrice, Nebraska and asked if John's father was a judge. With his confirmation she said, "We called him the marrying judge because of him being just across the state line and a lot of people of the allowed age eloped to see if he would perform their ceremony."

Memories of the Pulleine
Children in Home, Kansas

Marjorie	Patricia Ann	John	Margaret "Peg"
(Deceased)	*Alice is not in photo		**(Deceased)**

Alice Pulleine was the eldest child of Percy Pulleine and Gertrude Hamilton Pulleine. She was born on March 10, 1911 in Marysville. Alice attended grade school in Home, Kansas and graduated from Marysville High School in 1928. She attended normal class at Marysville High School and the teacher was Miss Garnet Hill. Alice qualified to teach and her first school was housed in a one room rock stone building one mile West of Blue Rapids at Hwy 77 at the entrance to West River Road.

Alice

And then she taught at the grade school in Home, Kansas. John Pulleine, her brother, remembers her being his teacher and that she passed him "on condition" that year.

Alice married an Annapolis graduate, Mann Hamm, and they had two sons and a daughter. Mann was stationed in Hawaii in December of 1941 and Alice and their children were living there. On that fateful weekend of December 7, 1941, a young ensign had taken Mann's weekend duty, voluntarily, so that Mann could be at home with his family. The young man was a casualty of the Japanese attack when the Oklahoma sank. Mann was at sea a lot over the years and Alice and their children would live in areas where his ship would dock from time to time. When Mann retired from the U.S. Navy as a Captain in the early 1950s the couple built a home in Pebble Beach, California on 17 Mile Drive and lived there until Alice died in 1986 at the age of 75.

Patricia Pulleine was the next child. Following graduation she worked in Marysville and later she worked in Salina, Kansas where she met James Douglass, a high school athletic director, and married him. They had a son and a daughter. Several years ago in answer to her early school days, Pat sent the following note: "I must have started to Home grade school in 1918 when I was six. The first school I attended was a one-room white building with a wood-burning stove in it. During the flu epidemic (of 1918 era) the school was closed but our mother kept up with Alice's and my schoolwork. As a result when we went back to school we both skipped a grade, going to two classes at once." Recall that their mother was a school teacher several years prior to marriage.

"My first teacher was Marie Keller, later Oehms, and I had a Miss Hadorn, Harley Prichard and Ralph Rohn as teachers until I finished the eighth grade in the spring of 1925."

Pat went on to say that Iola Ubben Albright, who lived in Hutchinson at that time, told her that she taught at District 42 from 1950 to 1952, with Ruth Ann Gurtler Flin.

Pat and Jim's son, James or Jimmy as he was known, lost his life in an automobile accident on his way home for Christmas and his parents' 25th wedding anniversary on Christmas Day in 1958. This was a terrible blow to his family and friends.—

Margaret "Peg" Pulleine was the third child of Percy and Gertrude and was born on July 20, 1917. Peg also married an Annapolis graduate, Ellis B. Rittenhouse, in 1936 and they were blessed with a son and a daughter. Peg's travels during her married life were much like Alice's. Alice and she each had a child born on the same day when they were both living in San Diego. When Ellis retired he was employed at the college in Corvallis, or where they lived for many years until his death. A 40-year resident of Corvallis, Peg thoroughly enjoyed golf, bridge, cooking, reading and traveling. "Her lifetime of commitments (including Good Samaritan Hospital Auxiliary and OSU Folk Club) stands as a shining example for all of us! We will never forget Peg's quick wit and dazzling smile!" She died December 2, 2006 in Citrus Heights, California after a long illness.

John William Pulleine, fourth child, was the only boy born in this family.

He seems to remember everything he did in school (or did not do) as well as being able to recall many names and associated memories. During WWII he was in the U.S. Navy and while stationed in Port Arthur, Texas he met and married Imogene Hamilton. After WWII he totally surprised her and his father by saying he planned for them to live in Texas and so they have. For the first forty years of their marriage the couple and their two daughters spent at least four long weekends in Kansas visiting John's father, Judge Percy Pulleine. And these trips always included a drive from Marysville to Home to visit friends and in later years just to see if there were more changes in the community.

John started to school in 1926, in Home's grade school, at six years of age and his early memories include having the freedom to run around town and do interesting things such as visit with the band of gypsies who camped near their home each Spring. He remembers that there was a tennis court at the school. He thinks he was fishing and swimming by the time he was six years old, sometimes without permission.

John's teachers were Fern Tangeman, 1st, 2nd, 3rd; Alice Pulleine, 4th; and Katie Kirch, 5th and 6th to the best of his recall. Allegedly Alice passed him "on condition" when he was a fourth grader.

Marjorie Louise Pulleine was the fifth child in this family whose twin

brother, Edwin, died twenty-four hours after birth. Marge started school in Home in 1928 according to her baby book record. Her baby book records the following teachers: Grade I (1928) Fern Tangeman; Grades 2 & 3 Alice Pulleine (her sister) and Grade 4 Adren Krouse. In 1932, when John was 12 and Marge was 11, their mother died and some time after that the family moved from Home to Marysville.

Marjorie remained a single person who moved to California in the early 1940's and when our country entered World War II, she went to work on an assignment with WARD as a civil service uniformed employee of the Army Air Corps in Hawaii. Marge described her workplace as a secret tunnel where they worked in conjunction with island placed radar stations that relayed information involving airplane and sea vessels locations to

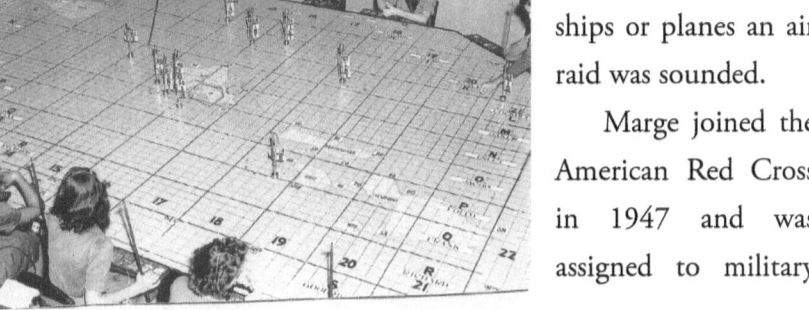

be plotted on a large grid marked map of the Islands. If activity was from unidentified ships or planes an air raid was sounded.

Marge joined the American Red Cross in 1947 and was assigned to military

45

installations in Japan, Korea, Austria, Germany, Scotland, Italy, and Guam as well as to some bases in the U.S.A She received commendation at her retirement at her retirement in 1984 after 37 years of service.

Marjorie Louise Pulleine died July 12, 2010 in San Antonio.

"There's No Place Like HOME"

For visitors it can become quite confusing to say "I am going home." So over the years many local residents started saying Home City at appropriate spots to distinguish the meaning between "home" and Home.

Rex

When John went to the service and Marge was living in California prior to the Women's Air Raid Service assignment in Hawaii, they faced the problem of their dog, Rex, having to be left alone. Rex was a Boston terrier and John and Marjorie's beloved pet.

Their father made arrangements with the butcher to have a charge account for Rex. This news made Ripley's Believe It Or Not. Rex made his daily calls to the butcher and at the end of the month, Dad received the charges and paid the bill.

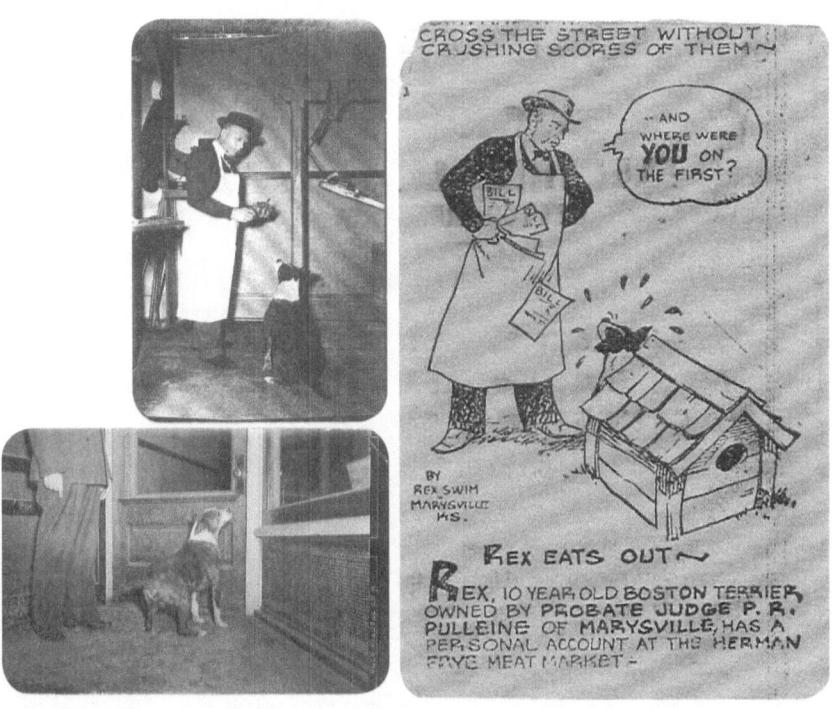

Letter from Percy Pulleine to John Pulleine In answer to a letter from John sharing thoughts of marriage

---

Marysville, Kansas

April 21, 1943

Dear John:

Enclosed find check that you can sign and return to me. I am enclosing my own check for $ 25.00. Your Security Benefit Life insurance premium is due and I will pay it. It is $ 15.05. I am very glad that you passed your Gunner's Mate examination with such good grades. Did you want me to return your certificate?

I am not surprised that you are considering marriage as it seems to be a disease that afflicts all men in service. However, it is a very serious step. You should be very sure, both of you, that you are fitted to go through life together. In the past you have not been very dependable and if married you will then not only have yourself to support, but a wife and, possibly, children. If you were to be stationed at one place, I would say, if you are certain the girl is the one you want, get married. But going to sea and possibly far-distant places and leaving behind a newly wedded wife, would not be wise. In a year or two of separation, the lady might meet someone who would supplant you in her affections, especially living in a community where she would come in contact with so many fine looking and desirable men and she then might regret her married state. The marriage vow is a very serious matter and you both should consider how will we feel towards each other 25 years from now; are we at this time willing to give in to each other, and do we trust one another? You have four fine sisters and should have an idea of the qualifications you would ask that your future wife have. You say she is neither good looking nor pretty. I suppose there is a distinction there. Well, neither is required in marriage. Is she clean minded, healthy, courteous and thoughtful of others? You see at my age I am rather out of touch with the present generation's ideas and thoughts. When I was your age every young fellow gave thought to his future wife's health, family connections, church, etc., knowing there would be, in those days, children. Your mother and I were not passionately in love with one another, but I knew she had all the qualifications any man could ask of his wife. I have always been proud of my good judgment. To you five, we gave perfect bodies and minds, yours to make or ruin when you went out on your own. Also, John, analyze yourself. You are too good looking for your own good. You have a bright mind—will you use it rightly? You are inclined to be selfish and to have a happy married life you will have to be the opposite. You have never saved any money until lately—will you keep saving?

When you were home on leave you spoke despairingly of Gene Tunney. I have lived and seen life and I will wager that, 40 years from now, those who speak thus will regret that they did not follow his advice. I hope, John that you will take this in the spirit in which it has been given and if you do get married, she will be my daughter.

I had another auto accident—hit by two boys who admit they never saw me, eight on Main Street, close to the curb. Badly hurt knee and cut o my shin. As usual I think I will come out o.k. Did you know that Mr. Longmire died? Doc seems to be getting along a little better and always asks about you.

The weather has been cold and variable and it freezes every night. I was very glad to get your letter as I had been watching every mail wondering why you had not written. I caught up with all my correspondence with the girls and now they all owe me letters. I had a letter from your Aunt Hazel the other day and she said Julian has a number of ships under his command now.

With best wishes for Easter. And how about attending services at some church on that day. Love, Dad

John & Imogene

During World War II, John Pulleine and Raul Perez became best friends. Raul Perez was from Houston, Texas. They were stationed in the Port Director's Office in Port Arthur, Texas. They were each gunner's mates and had attained their ranks while putting guns on the merchant ships so that the ships could transport the oil to the Europe war zones with some ability to defend their vessels.

Johnny was very handsome and a couple of girls were after him. Although John and I were courting at the time, the girls were still persistent. Raul, known to his friends as Porky, had a protective attitude towards me and on occasion helped me out with some of the negativity I received from other girls.

John and I met in January shortly after Christmas at a schedule dance at the Canteen. I had gone with a group of girls who urged me to go dance with John because he was the handsomest guy there. It was a girl's tag so I made a quick decision to just go ask him. Porky told me that the night John came home from the dance; John said to him "I found the girl I am going to marry." I had never had a steady boyfriend growing up so upon meeting John I advised him that I did not have steady relationships. However, within a couple of months he had convinced me that I should only date him and to my surprise, I was perfectly okay with it. It was a gradual thing with John and me. I received no flowers or extravagant things except for a silver cross he gave me. Then after some time, we talked about getting married.

Our wedding plans were originally made for Friday, September 17, 1943 to be held at St. George's Episcopal Church in Port Arthur, Texas. John made the arrangements for the ceremony. One of my best friends, Ruth Evelyn McDaniel, was to be maid of honor and John's roommate and friend, Raul Perez, was to be the best man. The marriage license and the blood test results, which were required to get married, were in John's hands. At that time there was a three day waiting period for the blood tests. Fortunately, that had been done and the application for the wedding license was made early. My parents and two brothers were at home at the time. Lowell Hamilton and George David Hamilton would be the only other people present at the wedding.

I had resigned from SW Bell Telephone Company and was employed by the Texaco Company. This change of employment was so that I could have day time working hours instead of the late hours I had been working.

John was a second class gunner's mate in the U.S. Navy and was detached to the Port Director's office in Port Arthur from Galveston and primarily from New Orleans, LA. John and Raul Perez had been roommates in Port Arthur for about six months and then Raul was moved back to Galveston. George Foley had been detected to Port Arthur and was a new roommate to John. While living off base they had to have quarters elsewhere and with shortages of housing local citizens rented bedrooms and such to military personnel.

Saturday, September 11, 1943 Imogene was scheduled for orientation at Texaco and was there for the day for a lengthy tour of the plant and paperwork. Communication was by telephone only and telephones were only in key offices. On that morning, John's commanding officer said to him, "I have orders for your immediate transfer and I hear that you are getting married next week. See you on Monday morning."

So John started trying to contact me with this news. My father worked for Texaco and endeavored to find my whereabouts in the plant during the tour. Finally about 3:00 p.m. when I left the plant I found John waiting for me. John told me the news and immediately the tears started falling and I was filled with dismay. A short while later it was decision making time for us. After all the "what ifs" were sifted through, we decided to try and arrange the wedding for that evening.

John had to pick up my ring at the jewelers and find a best man since Raul was in Galveston. I had to get a maid of honor since Ruth was in Baton Rouge, Louisiana. Probably my mother, Imogene Truett Hamilton, made the rest of the arrangements. She secured the minister and that, providentially, also provided the maid of honor, his daughter, Aline Williamson. Of course, by this time, these two titles for wedding attendants had been reduced to witnesses.

Long white dresses for weddings were unheard of during WWII. However, my mother had been sewing on a trousseau and making, first an ice blue light weight woolen dress as a model and a white dress in the same style. Since the white one was not completed, I had to wear the blue dress for my wedding. My father was working evenings at the time and was at work by then and my mother efficiently guided me through it all. She had called the minister and set that up, assisted me in dressing, packed a bag for me and probably heaved a big sigh as she watched us walk down the sidewalk. There had been no time for she and my brothers to get ready to go with us for this momentous occasion.

Memories of the ceremony itself include me crying from beginning to end, young Aline giggling intermittently, and George B. Foley saying several times, "I am not getting married until the war is over and then it will be a white wedding at the Cathedral in Boston." I wonder where he and his pompous attitude ended up.

John had rented a room from a widow lady in preparation of becoming a married man for him and me to live in. He made arrangements with her for us to have it a week early and secured the key for us to have that night. Plans had been made to go to a dance at the Pleasure Pier Ballroom and as soon as we were married we went from the ceremony to Pleasure

Pier Ballroom. With the announcement of our marriage to friends, congratulations and best wishes were conferred as John table hopped. Drinks were offered and there was dancing just like any other Saturday night. Then it was home for us, as bleary-weary as we were. On Sunday morning the lovely landlady set a beautiful bridal breakfast table with cut work table cloth, centerpiece, the best china, and made breakfast for the couple. The whole day was spent with John packing his belongings and tying up loose ends. One more night together and then John was off to Port Hueneme, California for his next duty station.

During the next three weeks I cried a lot, which was rather unusual for me, and I even lost fifteen pounds. When I returned from work one afternoon my parents surprised me by saying, "We have bought you a ticket from here (Beaumont, Texas) to Ventura, California. If you can be with John only a few days we know that you need to be with him while you can." My tears of misery turned to joyful tears at this announcement.

Packed with my clothes were sheets and pillowcases which I would need due to the shortages created by WWII. Three days later I was in Ventura and moving into a home provided by people whose daughter was in Marfa, Texas to be with her husband. The following day I applied for an operating position at the local telephone service and was employed on the spot. With a place to live, additional income and settling in for the duration, life was good.

Take a tip about being prepared ahead of time. If John had not already had the license and blood tests, maybe we wouldn't be celebrating our decades of marriage, 2 daughters, 2 grand-daughters, 1 grand-son, and 3 great grand-daughters. Appears that John was organized at that time in his life and after all this time, he still has that outstanding trait.

During the spring of 1944, John had a two week leave so we decided to go visit my new sister-in-laws. John and I rode the "Red Eye" from

Ventura to San Francisco and divided our time with five days in San Francisco with one sister, Alice Hamm and her three children who lived in a Victorian style house and five days with Margaret "Peg" Rittenhouse and her two children in Sausalito, California. We could see Alcatraz from Peg's living room window. Prior to this trip I had gone to see the doctor in Ventura. By then my pregnancy was confirmed and I braved the volume of entertainment, such as a couple of plays, "A Tree Grows in Brooklyn" and "Pirates of Penzance," that I enjoyed immensely.

One morning Alice and Peg took us to breakfast at "Top of the Mark" and then to a sale of diapers. With four of us gathered around we managed to come away with six dozen Birdseye diapers. Those diapers were of sturdy cloth and had a long life through our next child and some nieces & nephews who came along a bit later. On our arrival to Ventura, I returned to work. In July I took a leave of absent and traveled home to be with my parents until my baby was born with a due date of early November.

Maternity clothes were not easily available and if so were not well fitting and came in such ugly fabrics. Therefore, my mother made and designed maternity clothes for me. They fit perfectly and were really well designed. This was unusual for 1944, the year I was pregnant. I also remember my mother making one for my friend whom I took walks with so that we would not overheat.

Imogene Meets John's Father, 1945

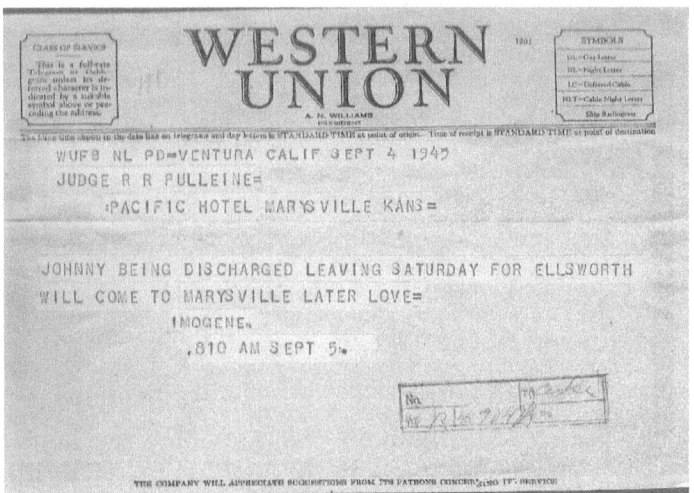

World War II, or WWII, as it has become known, ended in September of 1945 when the official papers were signed. Servicemen from all branches of USA's military were being released to return home. The order of discharge was based upon points attained for various criteria.

Though I do not remember exact dates my memories are based upon my experiences following this momentous process. John received orders to be discharged through Oakland, California.

At that time we were living in Ventura, California in a very small and relatively new garage apartment. Through friends, Ralph and Bobby Maxwell, we were loaned some furniture items. These items included an "ice box" (which was a former refrigerator of Bob and Ralph's), a card table, a couple of straight chairs, and a double bed. We had purchased a baby bed and a mattress for Candace or "Candy" as she was better known.

We also had a baby stroller that had been a gift from Ralph, Bob and friends.

Totally dismayed I let it be known, that I did not think that I could prepare and make the trip to my home all by myself. John explained, however, that military orders are ORDERS. So, he packed the requisite duffel bag and the next morning he left for his last duty of WWII and, ultimately, I packed and planned and did it alone.

At this point I thought about where I wanted to go. My parents had divorced shortly after Candy was born in 1944 and there was adequate space at Mom's. On the other side was the fact that I had not met John's father and another sister who lived in Ellsworth, Kansas. I flipped a switch in my brain and it clicked that I should take the train to Kansas and meet my father-in-law and another sister-in-law.

Our land lord crated the baby stroller and the household items I wanted to keep and took them to the train station nearby. I sold the baby bed and our friends picked up all the "loaners" we had been using. The day arrived, I boarded the train and at a long station stop in Tuscon, Arizona, a lady holding a gift package and a toy approached me. She was John's Aunt Agnes who lived in Tucson. The image in my memory is so vague because I was unaware that she would be there. That was the day of telegrams not e-mail or texting. Agnes Hamilton Martling was Gertrude's sister and kept in close touch with their mother who lived in Blue Rapids, Kansas.

My destination was reached and I stayed several days with Patricia Pulleine Douglass and her family in Ellsworth, Kansas. John's father drove to Ellsworth in his 1935 Plymouth Coupe to pick up Candace and I then went to Marysville, Kansas where my father-in-law resided. We found "gas ration stamps" from WWII in some of his family photos and papers. When we had settled into our hotel room, the old Pacific Hotel in Marysville, Kansas, we sat in the lobby and talked some more. Dad (he had instructed me to call him Dad as his own children did) advised me that he would babysit Candy, his grandchild, and had arranged for me to meet a group of John's friends from his high school days. Ultimately the group took me dancing with them but alas I did not know how to polka. I did however enjoy the "jitterbugging." I later learned that we had been at Turner Hall where John's mother and her friends had danced and John remembers sleeping on a bench there while all the people were dancing.

Two to three weeks later when John finally had been dismissed from military service and when he returned to Marysville, he was ready to socialize for a while and then settle. It was fun and Dad enjoyed the time with his grand daughter. One morning, a week or so later, John announced that he had tickets for us to go to my home. Dad commented, "Going to visit Imogene's parents now?" John replied, "We are going to live in Texas". Both his father and I were totally surprised.

This segues in to our life in Texas where we have lived during the balance of our married life. John earned an Associate Degree from Lamar University in Beaumont, Texas in 1947. We added another daughter, Robyn, in 1948. Each year, the four of us made three or four long week-end trips to visit with Dad until he departed this life in 1986.

While I was compiling this family story I asked my daughters what their favorite memory was of out trips to Kansas. Robyn's answer was: "You checking into motels on the way and in summer Candy, Daddy and I racing to change to suits for swimming". Also, she loved that old Pacific Hotel to play card games with Granddad and whoever was staying there for a few hours, railroad men, and strangers. Granddad taught Robyn how to play Canasta and other card games. Percy played Cribbage, Hearts, and Crazy Eights with both girls.

When I asked Candy what her favorite memories were of all our visits from Texas to Kansas to visit Dad she replied, "I liked going to the Courthouse and playing with his seal." Candy also said that she always enjoyed the long periods of time that she could read without being interrupted. Robyn was duly occupied with card games and John and I were off to his next designated visit to friends, or to have lunch and greet friends there.

52-20 Club

(1948-1949 Recession)

Some thought triggered a memory of one phase of John and my life together. Following the end of WWII servicemen returned home to either pick up their lives where they left off prior to being a member of the armed forces or to begin a new one. Jobs were at a premium and decisions were being made for living alternatives because of the Recession of 1948 to 1949. Our government devised a plan to assist financially until the men and women could establish a way of life for themselves and their family. It was referred to as the _52-20 Club_ because of the elements of the plan. Simply, for 52 weeks $20 was given to recipients who applied for the assistance and were approved.

John had used one of the other eligible assistance programs to go to college on the GI Bill and received a two year college certificate. Following this we returned to California to the area where he had been stationed during the last two years of WWII. I transferred from Southwestern Bell where I was a long distance operator to Pacific Telephone in California.

We had returned to Ventura, California and where we had friends we made from 1943-1945. For a year or so we lived in a small hotel near the beach while John looked for employment and took care of our three year old daughter while I was at work. We did not have a kitchen so we ate at all the local restaurants and frequently had smoked fish on the pier over the Pacific Ocean. Our entertainment was varied. John played cards with other hotel residents while I went to the movies and read. We went dancing with friends occasionally and John went out on a lobster boat sometimes with a friend. He took Candy, our three year old, with him everywhere he went.

Due to the fact we were living in this small, thirty-room hotel, brought about interaction with various types of people. There was a small group of musicians who made up an orchestra, a piano tuner who had a bar tab that he paid when need be by calling his customers to gather the money, a Russian couple with a baby, a single Russian lady and various people moving in and out. A lady owned the hotel and she had a young daughter. At Christmas she cooked a turkey and invited any of the hotel guests who wished to celebrate with her.

An outstanding event during this time was a Pacific storm that had huge waves and pounded our area of the coast for a couple of days. It created this repetitive *boom boom* sound which ultimately became annoying to me. When it ended word spread that a long sunken ship had been pushed ashore. People rushed to see this site and my most clear memory of it was the casks and chests and bolts of fabric that was still intact. We did not take any momentos but I think that some people did.

This way of life was during the Beatnik period and later when hippies were identified from the population by their approach to life, we had to admit that we had lived as Beatniks.

Just John

John's favorite clothing as a teenager was striped coveralls while in his teens. He spent a great deal of time at the Roundhouse and acquired a lot of information about the maintenance and scheduling of the trains. When he tired of hanging around there he climbed the steps up the steep hillside to his family's home on Caroline St. As adults he disliked costume parties however if he did honor us with his presence he dressed similar to the way railroad engineers dressed when on maintenance duty. Even though we grew up during the 1930's Depression, John was employed for several years as an usher at the movie theatre. His memory is still excellent and he can still recite the movie stars who were in many black and white and later

color movies. Excellent if it appears in a Trivia game.

The year that he was sixteen he spent the summer in Topeka, Kansas as page in the Kansas Senate.

Later, back home, he worked with the local funeral director and he and his best friend did the necessary driving required. His friend, Francis Long, later purchased the mortuary, married a young lady who became his helpmate for the various volunteer counseling requirements.

John is listed as a member of the Spanish Club for the 1938 graduation class of Marysville High School and though he can not converse in Spanish he still knows many of the words and we keep a Spanish dictionary nearby if we need to see how a word is spelled.

Shrimp Boat Owner

When we lived in Port Arthur, Texas John Pulleine and two friends, Jack Hardin and Hart Basana, decided that they would like to have a shrimp boat (for deep sea fishing for Red Snapper.) It is not known how the idea was formed or how long it grew before they bought the desired boat.

They located a boat for sale that was docked at Avery Island in Louisiana. The route for taking the boat from there to Port Arthur was the Intercoastal Canal. These three intrepid fellows went to the Coast Guard in Port Arthur and procured a map of the waterway they would be sailing the shrimp boat on. John drove, with his friends, from home to Avery Island and Jack and Hart sailed the boat home with John following their route in his car.

My memories of the time the fellows were gone was that one of the wives called several times and was frantic because she hadn't heard from her husband. She proposed going to look for them. There were two daughters in the Pulleine household, one was in elementary school and the other was in junior high school, and Imogene never left them alone so it was not a thing she would do. The other wife did not contact Imogene and to tell the truth Imogene was not concerned about the fellows because she felt that they were resourceful. After all, they shared a variety of talents.

Meanwhile the fellows were happily sailing along, going aground a couple of times and having to wait for the tide to rise to be able to sail again, and having coffee with the ferry keepers. They arrived home in due time and docked their prized possession near Orange, Texas. Then for a couple of years or so they spent all their days off from their regular jobs working to restore the boat. Allegedly, during that time they took the boat out on to Lake Sabine one time. Truth to tell, they might just have had fun cleaning it up.

Then John took a new job in 1959 and we moved to La Porte, Texas so the three of them eventually found a buyer and sold the boat. It was a fun time for the fellows and assuredly they were using their off time well. This vintage cypress hull boat was tawdry looking when they found it and it emerged restored to a near likeness of its original presentation.

This photo is of a watercolor by Michael Case painted in the 1950's when he was in college at Lamar University. It had been on loan to Imogene for years. Prior to returning it to Mike, Imogene photographed it because it reminded her of the shrimp boat John had once held a third interest in.

Village Creek, Texas near Beaumont

After church in Beaumont

Alas, Divorce

I have to be honest and tell you that after many years of managing our lives together and rearing two wonderful daughters who laughed at our way of arguing and within a few minutes going on to something new. The arguments were sometimes fierce statements. Finally we used the word *divorce* and then we discussed disposition of property. My parents had divorced in 1944 and remarried in 1948 and I did remember how bad she felt in her abandonment.

So, at one point we consulted an attorney and paperwork was put into the system. Our divorce was final in June, 1964.

Robyn and I were still living in our house. John was living in an efficiency apartment a few miles from us. Candy was living in a dorm at Lamar University in Beaumont, Texas where she was a sophomore. Except for work at the doctor's office, Robyn's activities, and my membership meetings, I rarely left our house. Then about six months later, after the Christmas holiday and John and the girls had been gone for two weeks for a Kansas visit, I resumed social activities in our community. Friends called and I attended a couple of parties. After New Years, John and I met and talked, talked, and talked and made the decision to see each other, and agreed to marry again when we had spent an entire weekend together without an argument.

Our friends and my family had not taken us seriously and some played jokes on us and my mother would say, "You kids might as well get married again as much time as you spend together now." This was her comment a couple of times when she found me on an overnighter with John.

The day of no arguments arrived when John and I had spent a long weekend together in Lake Charles, Louisiana and I realized that we had not had an argument. We were almost home when I mentioned it to him. He said, "Great, now set the date one more time".

To keep it a secret, except from the girls and a few friends, we went to the neighboring county, Liberty, Texas and applied for the marriage license. Without fanfare we were seated in a pew at St. John's Episcopal Church, La Porte, Texas; Candy and Robyn and a few guests were seated in the choir section behind the pulpits. Rev. Raish, now deceased, performed our marriage ceremony on July 10, 1965. During this ceremony, second time around, our daughters performed the giggling act and I smiled

instead of showering tears. Burlen and Audrey Griffith, friends, were our witnesses and surprised us with a lovely party at their home following the ceremony.

John and I have always celebrated our original wedding date following the divorce and remarriage. I had to search for the marriage certificate to verify the date of the second marriage and found that it is around the time Robyn and Dail got married. They were married by a Justice of the Peace who lived nearby. It was on July 7th in 1971. Dail was happy that Robyn had had a formal wedding at St. John's Episcopal Church the first time around and Robyn said that she just wanted it to be the two of them for this marriage.

Happy note: They had one son, and he did not get married until he was thirty-five and he met and married a young lady of approximately the same age. Their story is of internet romance.

One of Rodney's friends gave him a gift on a site to meet someone. Rodney dated a lot, went to clubs with his two older sisters and their dates and anyone he was dating at the time. He just was not serious about anyone. His friend kept asking Rodney if he had used his gift. Consequently, he met a young lady and then another. His second date, Lori, is now John's and my granddaughter-in-law and fantastic. When they had some more dates they each agreed to participate in at least one of their favorite activities. Rodney agreed to go to concerts and plays and Lori agreed to go fishing and hunting. That meant wearing suits for Rodney, to his discontent, and Lori having to add hunting camouflage items to her wardrobe.

Rodney and Lori had a beautiful wedding and reception. For the garter aspect of the reception Lori's mother said to me, "Imogene you are going to love this." Rodney on bended knee, groping for a garter, looked up in surprise and raised Lori's skirt a bit higher. Lori then lifted her wedding dress skirt to reveal camouflage boots. This was no surprise but was very funny. All the groomsmen had duck callers and at many points during the reception, it was "Quack, quack."

These two were surprised that Lori was pregnant the following year. That child is now two years of age and is so sassy that she was on the verge of being dismissed from her play school. When they put her in the three year old group she became a happy camper. This marriage is one of those happy internet meetings resulting in a great marriage.

The compilation of Taffinder and Julia is from one of their sons, Percy Ronald Vail Pulleine, and his daughter-in-law, Imogene includes more information about several generations of descendants. This information is from numerous years of research by their ancestors and in some cases their siblings.

Each family researcher's contact with successive generation family members elicited various answers. Reactions varied from personal lack of interest to their children lacking an interest in their family history thus creating reluctance to share their information. Twenty years ago, research involved trips to ancestors past family former resident courthouses, cemeteries, and churches.

This is a family who spent WWII during the early 1940's and shortly after the Korean Conflict during the early 1950's, hundreds of miles apart from their aunts, uncles, and cousins. They settled in areas where they had grown up.

Today's technology and many hours of genealogy volunteer work using the internet now opens access to censuses, abstracts of many categories for vital research, published family trees, and related maps. There are many other avenues open for advanced research for individuals.

I leave you the clues present in the Appendix to help you gather information if you need it.

Appendix

The modified register system is basically a listing of all persons in a given generation. Every child is assigned a number and persons who are continued in the next generation have a plus sign (+) next to their number. The appendix is from a data entry of descendants of Taffinder and Julia. It has brief explanations of how to read and assimilate order positions in family.

Descendants of
William Taffinder Pulleine and Juliana Julia Dunn

1. **William Taffinder**[1] **Pulleine**, born 8 Jan 1843 in Drax Hall, near Shelby, Yorkshire, England; died 30 Sep 1911 in Marysville, Marshall County, Kansas, son of William Pulleine and Mary Twigg. He married on 31 Mar 1870 in Patrington, Yorkshire, England **Juliana Julia Dunn**, born 10 Jul 1843; died 20 Apr 1914 in Marysville, Marshall County, Kansas, U.S.A., daughter of Isaac Dunn and Mary Jane Raines.

Notes for William Taffinder Pulleine
    From the data entry from Imogene's research

<u>Notes for Juliana Julia Dunn</u>

From the data entry from Imogene's research

Children of William Taffinder Pulleine and Juliana Julia Dunn were as follows:

2 i **Hilda Muriel Zoe**[2] **Pulleine**, born Abt Dec 1870 or Jan 1871 in Virginia; died 10 Sep 1874 in Marysville, Marshall County, Kansas. Notes: From Pulleine-Dunn family history by Earle Frost. Died at age 3 years and 9 months of age.

3 ii **Guy Addison**[2] **Pulleine**, born 29 Dec 1871 in Virginia, USA; died 29 Jul 1932 in Marysville, Marshall County, Kansas. Notes: From the Pulleine-Dunn family history by Earle Frost. Different birth year on Guy's tombstone causing conflict in information. Earle's information was transcribed from information his mother had gathered and from a diary that had been kept by Julia Dunn Pulleine's mother (copy in possession of Earle Frost) and is more likely to be accurate.

+ 4 iii **Myrtle Mary**[2] **Pulleine**, born 3 Mar 1876; died 6 Nov 1947. She married **John Frost**.

5 iv **Samuel Taffinder**[2] **Pulleine**, born 7 Feb 1878 in Marysville, Marshall County, Kansas; died 17 May 1945 in Marysville, Marshall County, Kansas. Notes: From the Pulleine-Dunn family history by Earle Frost.

+ 6 v **Percy Ronald Vail**[2] **Pulleine**, born 23 Nov 1880 in Marshall County, Kansas; died 29 Sep 1976 in Marysville, Marshall County, Kansas. He married **Gertrude May Hamilton**.

+ 7 vi **Violet Hyacinth**[2] **Pulleine**, born 31 Oct 1882; died 5 Nov 1969. She married **Charles John Daniel Koester**.

8   vii   **Beatrix Mabel Ivy**[2] **Pulleine**, born 6 Nov 1888; died 20 Jul 1899. Notes: From the Pulleine-Dunn family history by Earle Frost.

Generation 2

4. **Myrtle Mary**[2] **Pulleine** (William Taffinder[1]), born 3 Mar 1876; died 6 Nov 1947. She married on 28 Dec 1896 in Kansas **John Frost**, born 6 Jan 1874; died 19 Jan 1953.

Notes for Myrtle Mary Pulleine

From the Pulleine-Dunn family history by Earle Frost.

Children of Myrtle Mary Pulleine and John Frost were as follows:

+ 9   i   **Clyde Dow**[3] **Frost**, born 27 Oct 1897. He married **Mary Claudys Miller**.

+ 10   ii   **Earle Wesley**[3] **Frost**, born 11 Jul 1899. He married **Esther Christenson Houston**.

+ 11   iii   **Dorothy Mabel**[3] **Frost**, born 23 May 1901. She married **Harry Herbert Halbower**.

+ 12   iv   **Hilda Hyacinth**[3] **Frost**, born 29 Oct 1903 in Blue Rapids, Marshall County, Kansas; died 25 Aug 1999 in West Pennsylvanialm Beach, Florida. She married **Jack Wilbur Dunlap**.

13   v   **Ruth Isabel**[3] **Frost**, born 2 Aug 1906. She married **Keith Donald Larson**, born 14 Apr 1908.

14   vi   **Virgil Esther**[3] **Frost**, born 24 Dec 1907. She married **Eugene Frederick Laubengayer**, born 1 Jan 1905.

15   vii   **Frances Mary (Jane)**[3] **Frost**, born 5 Apr 1913. She married **Ellsworth Eugene, Jr. Empie**, born 1 Jan 1910.

6. **Percy Ronald Vail**[2] **Pulleine** (William Taffinder[1]), born 23 Nov 1880 in Marshall County, Kansas; died 29 Sep 1976 in Marysville, Marshall County, Kansas. He married in Sep 1909 in, Marshall County, Kansas **Gertrude May Hamilton**, born 16 Sep 1885 in Blue Rapids, Marshall County, Kansas; died 27 Jul 1932 in Marysville, Marshall County, Kansas, daughter of John Lafayette Hamilton and Alice Fitzgerald.

Notes for Gertrude May Hamilton

From obituary. From Pulleine-Dunn family history written by Earle Frost.

Children of Percy Ronald Vail Pulleine and Gertrude May Hamilton were as follows:

+ 16   i   **Alice Julia**[3] **Pulleine**, born 10 Mar 1911 in Home, Marshall County, Kansas; died 2 Apr 1986 in Monterey, California. She married **Mann Leander Hamm**.

+ 17   ii   **Patricia Ann**[3] **Pulleine**, born 17 Jul 1912 in Marysville, Marshall County, Kansas. She married **James McNair Douglass**.

+ 18   iii   **Margaret Chloe**[3] **Pulleine**, born 20 Jul 1917; died 2 Dec 2006 in Sacramento, CA. She married **Ellis Brooks Rittenhouse Sr.**

+ 19   iv   **John William**[3] **Pulleine**, born 7 Jun 1920 in Home, Marshall County, Kansas. He married **Imogene Hamilton**.

20   v   **Edwin Guy³ Pulleine**, born 11 Feb 1922; died 11 Feb 1922. Notes: From the Pulleine-Dunn family history and from known information.

21   vi   **Marjory Louise³ Pulleine**, born 11 Feb 1922: died 12 July 2010. Notes: From the Pulleine-Dunn family history and also known information.

7. **Violet Hyacinth² Pulleine** (William Taffinder¹), born 31 Oct 1882; died 5 Nov 1969. She married **Charles John Daniel Koester**, born 9 Jun 1881; died 9 Oct 1965 in Marysville, Marshall County, Kansas.

Notes for Violet Hyacinth Pulleine

From the Pulleine-Dunn family history by Earle Frost.

Children of Violet Hyacinth Pulleine and Charles John Daniel Koester were as follows:

+ 22   i   **Charles William³ Koester**, born 3 Feb 1909 in Marysville, Kansas, USA; died 12 Jan 2005 in Prairie Village, Kansas, USA. He married **Sarah Ellen Snipes**.

+ 23   ii   **Julia Constance³ Koester**, born 3 Nov 1911. She married **Richard Weldon King**.

Generation 3

9. **Clyde Dow³ Frost** (Myrtle Mary² Pulleine, William Taffinder¹), born 27 Oct 1897. He married **Mary Claudys Miller**, born 3 Jan 1903; died 14 Jul 1974.

Children of Clyde Dow Frost and Mary Claudys Miller were as follows:

24   i   **Clyde Raymond**[4] **Frost**, born 27 May 1933; died 27 May 1933.

25   ii   **Lois Ruth**[4] **Frost**, born 14 Oct 1934.

10. **Earle Wesley**[3] **Frost** (Myrtle Mary[2] Pulleine, William Taffinder[1]), born 11 Jul 1899. He married **Esther Christenson Houston**, born 18 Jul 1899.

Children of Earle Wesley Frost and Esther Christenson Houston were as follows:

+ 26   i   **Earle Wesley, Jr**[4] **Frost**, born 14 Mar 1933. He married (1) unknown; (2) **Dorie Lee Stites** (see 47).

11. **Dorothy Mabel**[3] **Frost** (Myrtle Mary[2] Pulleine, William Taffinder[1]), born 23 May 1901. She married **Harry Herbert Halbower**, born 5 Jun 1899.

Children of Dorothy Mabel Frost and Harry Herbert Halbower were as follows:

27   i   **Jane Louise**[4] **Halbower**, born 13 Jan 1929.

28   ii   **Harry Herbert, Jr.**[4] **Halbower**, born 29 Oct 1931; died 10 Sep 1955. He married **Virginia Lou Stark**.

12. **Hilda Hyacinth**[3] **Frost** (Myrtle Mary[2] Pulleine, William Taffinder[1]), born 29 Oct 1903 in Blue Rapids, Marshall County, Kansas; died 25 Aug 1999 in West Pennsylvania Beach, Florida. She married **Jack Wilbur Dunlap**, born 11 Aug 1902; died 8 May 1977.

Children of Hilda Hyacinth Frost and Jack Wilbur Dunlap were as follows:

29   i   **Jack William**[4] **Dunlap**, born 19 Dec 1924. He married **Neoma Shaw**, born 25 Oct 1925.

16. **Alice Julia**[3] **Pulleine** (Percy Ronald Vail[2], William Taffinder[1]), born 10 Mar 1911 in Home, Marshall County, Kansas; died 2 Apr 1986 in Monterey, California. She married on 31 Mar 1933 in Yuma, AZ **Mann Leander Hamm**, born 24 Jun 1909 in Bellevue, Texas; died 28 May 2001 in Monterrey CA.

Notes for Alice Julia Pulleine

Some information is from the Pulleine-Dunn family history by Earle Frost. (P.R. Pulleine, her father furnished the information to Earle from his family records)

Alice was a grade school teacher in Home, Kansas for several years and had John, brother, and Marjorie, sister in her classes. John has said, laughingly, "Alice passed me on condition when I was in the fourth grade."

From The Marysville Advocate, April 34, 1997, page 7B: It Happened Here, by Oretha Ruetti. One of the paragraphs dealt with a 10-week contest which had News readers searching for intentionally misspelled words in advertisements and Miss Alice Pulleine won the contest. It was in 1927 and the theme was Home Beautiful Project.

Alice allegedly was an avid watcher of "Wheel of Fortune" and had an interest in cross word puzzles.

Social Security Index: Information appears to be correct.

Ashes cast at sea, off Pebble Beach California (personal residence for more than 30 years.)

Notes for Mann Leander Hamm

Obituary in the Monterey County Herald, Sunday, June 3, 2001:

Stated that "he was born June 24, 1909 in Bellevue, Texas.

Graduated from the U.S. Naval Academy in 1931 and attended Naval Postgraduate School in 1935-1937. He served on the USS Oklahoma until the vessel sank in the Japanese raid on Pearl Harbor.

In a note in his 1999 Christmas card from Mann: "Am 90 (24 June 99)-birthday in obituary same after calculation made.

Thank you note from son, July 19, 2001: Dearest John & Imogene,

Thank you for your kind memorial gift to the hospice. The Coast Guard dispersed Mann's ashes off the coast to join Les and Mother (Alice).

We (Leslie's children and I) had a picnic and a time to complete ourselves with Dad as well as Lee, Mom and Les. It's been quality time. Love, Michael Hamm

Children of Alice Julia Pulleine and Mann Leander Hamm were as follows:

30   i   **Lee Robert**[4] **Hamm**, born 5 Dec 1934; died 19 Apr 1990 in Monterey, California. Notes: Bachelor like a few of the Pulleine males. And, when the Pulleines are widowed the men nor the women seem to remarry. Like a tradition.

31   ii   **Michael Richard**[4] **Hamm**, born 5 Dec 1938 in Long Beach,, California.

+ 32   iii   **Leslie Ann**[4] **Hamm**, born 21 Apr 1940 in Long Beach, California; died 6 Feb 1989 in San Luis Obispo, California. She married **Dave Lynn Englund**.

17. **Patricia Ann**[3] **Pulleine** (Percy Ronald Vail[2], William Taffinder[1]), born 17 Jul 1912 in Marysville, Marshall County, Kansas. She married on 24 Dec 1932 in St. Pennsylvaniaul's Episcopal Church, Marysville, Kansas **James McNair Douglass**, born 26 Aug 1902; died in July 1985.

Notes for Patricia Ann Pulleine

Taken from the Pulleine-Dunn family history by Earle Frost. Also, known information.

Children of Patricia Ann Pulleine and James McNair Douglass were as follows:

33   i   **James McNair**[4] **Douglass Jr**, born 23 Oct 1935 in, Kansas; died 24 Dec 1957.

+ 34   ii   **Mary Patricia**[4] **Douglass**, born 1938 in Concordia, Kansas. She married **John Edward Dunlop**.

18. **Margaret Chloe³ Pulleine** (Percy Ronald Vail², William Taffinder¹), born 20 Jul 1917; died 2 Dec 2006 in Sacramento, CA. She married on 29 Aug 1936 in Marysville, Marshall County, Kansas **Ellis Brooks Rittenhouse Sr**, born 14 Nov 1912; died Jul 1978.

Notes for Margaret Chloe Pulleine

Taken from the Pulleine-Dunn family history by Earle Frost. Also, known information.

Children of Margaret Chloe Pulleine and Ellis Brooks Rittenhouse Sr were as follows:

+ 35 i   **Ellis Brooks⁴ Rittenhouse Jr**, born 21 Apr 1940. He married **Katherine Jane Laughton**.
+ 36 ii   **Susan Pulleine⁴ Rittenhouse**, born 21 Jul 1941. She married **Charles Marvin Everest**.

19. **John William³ Pulleine** (Percy Ronald Vail², William Taffinder¹), born 1920 in Home, Marshall County, Kansas. He married on 11 Sep 1943 in Port Arthur, Jefferson County, Texas **Imogene Hamilton**, born 1923 in Lafayette, Louisiana, daughter of Christopher John 'June' Hamilton and Imogene 'Sis' Truett.

Notes for Imogene Hamilton

Birth Certificate, marriage certificate.

Proofs of most of the ancestors information that appear in this book have been attained at the time of research for all the applications for membership in patriotic, or lineage, organizations. Presently, is a member of the Daughters of the American Revolution, Daughters of the Republic of Texas, Daughters of the War of 1812, and United Daughters of the Confederacy. Curiousity and a sense of family pride evolved into an objective to establish published facts regarding the role the ancestors held in creating the State of Texas. It is hoped that this factual information can now be a basis for future generations to study their family history.

Children of John William Pulleine and Imogene Hamilton were as follows:

37　i　**Candace Vale**[4] **Pulleine**, born 1944 in Port Arthur, Jefferson County, Texas. She married on 2 Sep 1967 in La Porte, Harris County, Texas, divorced **Floyd Harper Jr.**, born 1943 in Jasper, Texas, son of Floyd B Harper Sr. and Artie Rae Clark. Notes: Birth date Information is from birth certificate on file with family. Attended Lamar University in Beaumont, Texas for two years. There she met Floyd Harper, Jr. and they were married on September 2, 1967. Wedding at St. John's Episcopal Church, La Porte, Texas and the reception was held at the home of her parents, 10219 Carlow Lane, La Porte, Texas. Divorced Spril 27, 1970.

+ 38　ii　**Robyn Lane**[4] **Pulleine**, born 1948 in Port Arthur, Jefferson County, Texas. She married (1) **Timothy Harmon Jones**; (2) **Rodney Dail Blackman Jr.**

22. **Charles William**[3] **Koester** (Violet Hyacinth[2] Pulleine, William Taffinder[1]), born 3 Feb 1909 in Marysville, Kansas, USA; died 12 Jan 2005 in Prairie Village, Kansas, USA. He married on 21 Nov 1942 **Sarah Ellen Snipes**, born 2 Mar 1914.

Children of Charles William Koester and Sarah Ellen Snipes were as follows:

39   i   **Charles William**[4] **Koester**, born 1945. He married **Constance Sue Smith**, born 1945.

40   ii   **Sarah Pruden**[4] **Koester**, born 1947. She married **James Remmers, Jr. Brigham**, born 1945.

41   iii   **Julia Wills**[4] **Koester**, born 25 Mar 1949; died 26 Apr 1949.

42   iv   **John Daniel**[4] **Koester**, born 1951.

43   v   **Broughten Pulleine**[4] **Koester**, born 1953. He married **Marilyne Daniel Tron**, born 1952.

23. **Julia Constance**[3] **Koester** (Violet Hyacinth[2] Pulleine, William Taffinder[1]), born 3 Nov 1911. She married **Richard Weldon King**, born 1 Jan 1912; died 11 Oct 1952.

Children of Julia Constance Koester and Richard Weldon King were as follows:

44   i   **Richard Koester**[4] **King**, born 19 Oct 1940; died 6 Nov 1940.

45   ii   **Julia Janie**[4] **King**, born 14 Nov 1941. She married **Jon David Muller**, born 1941.

+ 46   iii   **Richard Charles**[4] **King**, born 1944. He married **Judith Lynn Brown**.

Generation 4

26. **Earle Wesley, Jr**[4] **Frost** (Earle Wesley[3], Myrtle Mary[2] Pulleine, William Taffinder[1]), born 14 Mar 1933. He married (1) unknown; (2) ?? **Dorie Lee Stites** (see 47), born 27 Mar 1933, daughter of Earle Wesley, Jr Frost.

Children of Earle Wesley, Jr Frost were as follows:

47   i   **Dorie Lee**[5] **Stites**, born 1933. She married ?? **Earle Wesley, Jr Frost** (see 26), born 1933, son of Earle Wesley Frost and Esther Christenson Houston.

Children of Earle Wesley, Jr Frost and Dorie Lee Stites were as follows:

48   i   **Leiegh Carol**[5] **Frost**, born 1956.
49   ii   **Laura Jane**[5] **Frost**, born 1957.
50   iii **Lisabeth Ann**[5] **Frost**, born 1960.
51   iv   **John Lawrence**[5] **Frost**, born 1963.

32. **Leslie Ann**[4] **Hamm** (Alice Julia[3] Pulleine, Percy Ronald Vail[2], William Taffinder[1]), born 21 Apr 1940 in Long Beach, California; died 6 Feb 1989 in San Luis Obispo, California. She married, divorced Dave **Lynn Englund**, born 25 Jul 1934.

Notes for Leslie Ann Hamm

Birth and death information is from her family members. Leslie attended college in Hawaii and married there. She was divorced after having three children and became a single mother who worked hard, played with her children and enjoyed her hobbies. Primarily she loved horses and had one of her own. Her children held a wonderful Celebration of Life for her memorial following her request. She fought a courageous battle with Cancer before losing.

Birth and death dates are verified in Social Security Index.

Children of Leslie Ann Hamm and Dave Lynn Englund were as follows:

+ 52 i   **Kirsten April**[5] **Englund**, born 1961. She married **Ford James**.
+ 53 ii   **Erin Heather**[5] **Englund**, born 1962. She married **David Fleishman**.
+ 54 iii   **Matthew Aaron**[5] **Englund**, born 1965. He married **Stephanie Knight**.

34. **Mary Patricia**[4] **Douglass** (Patricia Ann[3] Pulleine, Percy Ronald Vail[2], William Taffinder[1]), born 1938 in Concordia, Kansas. She married **John Edward Dunlop**, born 14 Jul 1935.

Children of Mary Patricia Douglass and John Edward Dunlop were as follows:

55 i   **James Douglass**[5] **Dunlop**, born 1967.
56 ii   **Catherine Anne**[5] **Dunlop**, born 1968.

35. Ellis Brooks[4] **Rittenhouse Jr** (Margaret Chloe[3] Pulleine, Percy Ronald Vail[2], William Taffinder[1]), born 1940. He married **Katherine Jane Laughton**, born 1941.

Children of Ellis Brooks Rittenhouse Jr and Katherine Jane Laughton were as follows:

57   i   **David Laughton**[5] **Rittenhouse**, born 1966.
58   ii   **Andrew Pulleine**[5] **Rittenhouse**, born 1968.

36. Susan Pulleine[4] **Rittenhouse** (Margaret Chloe[3] Pulleine, Percy Ronald Vail[2], William Taffinder[1]), born 21 Jul 1941. She married, divorced **Charles Marvin Everest**, born 1942.

Children of Susan Pulleine Rittenhouse and Charles Marvin Everest were as follows:

+ 59 i   **Pamela Wilson**[5] **Everest**, born 1963. She married **Leonard Melton**.

38. Robyn Lane[4] **Pulleine** (John William[3], Percy Ronald Vail[2], William Taffinder[1]), born 1948 in Port Arthur, Jefferson County, Texas. She married (1) on 19 May 1967 in La Porte, Harris County, Texas, divorced Timothy **Harmon Jones**, born 16 Apr 1948 in Oceanside, San Diego County, California; died 6 Oct 2008 in Phoenix Arizona, son of Robert Henry Jones and Katherine Crawshaw Watt; (2) in 1971 in Louisiana Porte, Harris County, Texas **Rodney Dail Blackman Jr.**, born 1945 in Houston, Harris County, Texas, son of Rodney Dail Blackman Sr. and Lucy Fay Jury.

Notes for Robyn Lane Pulleine

Information from birth & marriage certificates and final decree of divorce.

Notes for Timothy Harmon Jones

Mother's maiden name: Katherine Crawshaw Watt (from birth certificate abstract) Father's name: Robert Henry Jones (same as above)

Certified Abstract of Birth from San Diego County Recorder: 7-29-1991

Will be in possession of either Catherine Jones Allison or Elizabeth Jones Ueding.

First marriage date to Ruana (California) is from Ancestry.com's Index: California marriages

There is a second marriage record on Ancestry.com's Index: Texas Marriages and is 30 June 1972

Tim's Jones ancestors are from Eric Robertson Jones (his brother's) PAF Pedigree and Individual information entries

Notes for Rodney Dail Blackman Jr.

Information from family records.

Children of Robyn Lane Pulleine and Timothy Harmon Jones were as follows:

+ 60 i   **Elizabeth Anne**[5] **Jones**, born 1967 in Channelview, Harris County, Texas. She married **Gregory Allen Ueding**.

+ 61 ii **Catherine Jana**[5] **Jones**, born 1969 in Channelview, Harris County, Texas. She married (1) **Zoltan Eric McVeigh**; (2) **Daryl Lance Allison**.

Children of Robyn Lane Pulleine and Rodney Dail Blackman Jr. were as follows:

+ 62 i **Rodney Dail**[5] **Blackman III**, born 1972 in Houston, Harris County, Texas. He married **Lori Ann Nelson**.

46. **Richard Charles**[4] **King** (Julia Constance[3] Koester, Violet Hyacinth[2] Pulleine, William Taffinder[1]), born 1944. He married **Judith Lynn Brown**, born 1944.

Children of Richard Charles King and Judith Lynn Brown were as follows:

63 i **Brian Charles**[5] **King**, born 1974. He married **Catherine Elizabeth**, born 1977.

Generation 5

52. **Kirsten April**[5] **Englund** (Leslie Ann[4] Hamm, Alice Julia[3] Pulleine, Percy Ronald Vail[2], William Taffinder[1]), born 1961. She married **Ford James**.

Children of Kirsten April Englund and Ford James were as follows:

64 i **Robin Liam**[6] **James**, born 1995 in Juneau, Alaska.

53. Erin Heather[5] **Englund** (Leslie Ann[4] Hamm, Alice Julia[3] Pulleine, Percy Ronald Vail[2], William Taffinder[1]), born 1962. She married **David Fleishman**.

Children of Erin Heather Englund and David Fleishman were as follows:

65   i   **Kylan Matthew**[6] **Fleishman**, born 1997.

54. Matthew Aaron[5] **Englund** (Leslie Ann[4] Hamm, Alice Julia[3] Pulleine, Percy Ronald Vail[2], William Taffinder[1]), born 1965. He married in 1997 in California **Stephanie Knight**.

Children of Matthew Aaron Englund and Stephanie Knight were as follows:

66   i   **Lucas Eschan**[6] **Englund**, born 1997 in California.

59. Pamela Wilson[5] **Everest** (Susan Pulleine[4] Rittenhouse, Margaret Chloe[3] Pulleine, Percy Ronald Vail[2], William Taffinder[1]), born 1963. She married in Oregon **Leonard Melton**.

Children of Pamela Wilson Everest and Leonard Melton were as follows:

67   i   **Stephanie**[6] **Melton**, born 1981 in Oregon.
68   ii   **Kaylee**[6] **Melton**, born 1994 in Oregon.

60. **Elizabeth Anne⁵ Jones** (Robyn Lane⁴ Pulleine, John William³, Percy Ronald Vail², William Taffinder¹), born 1967 in Channelview, Harris County, Texas. She married on 1 Apr 1995 in La Porte, Harris County, Texas, divorced **Gregory Allen Ueding**, born 1968 in Newton, Jasper County, Iowa, son of Ralph Ueding and Linda Diane King.

Notes for Elizabeth Anne Jones
Information from birth certificate and self.

Notes for Gregory Allen Ueding
Linda, Greg's mother, married a second time to David Lynn Rogers. David was and is his nurturing father.

Information regarding Gregory's marriage to Molly A. Jameyson and Sara and Matt's b.d.'s from the Texas Marriage and the Texas Divorce Indexes

Children of Elizabeth Anne Jones and Gregory Allen Ueding were as follows:

69   i   **Madison Dayn⁶ Ueding**, born 1999 in Houston, Harris County, Texas. Notes: Madison's middle name was made up by her mother, Elizabeth, using the first two letters of Dail Blackman and Robyn Pulleine Blackman (DAYN)

61. **Catherine Jana⁵ Jones** (Robyn Lane⁴ Pulleine, John William³, Percy Ronald Vail², William Taffinder¹), born 1969 in Channelview, Harris County, Texas. She married (1) on 11 Dec 1987 in Clear Lake City, Harris County, Texas, divorced **Zoltan Eric McVeigh**, born 1968 in Houston,

Harris County, Texas; (2) on 17 Mar 1995 in Galveston, Galveston County, Texas **Daryl Lance Allison**, born 1969 in Beaumont, Jefferson County, Texas, son of John Wayne Allison and Virginia Lee Wolcik.

Notes for Catherine Jana Jones

Information from family records and self.

Copy of birth certificate.

Membership approved in Daughters of the Republic of Texas (DRT), Daughters of the American Revolution (DAR), Daughters of the War of 1812, Indian Wars, Mayflower Descendants. Lineage documents submitted approved by all.

Notes for Zoltan Eric McVeigh

Information from birth and marriage certificates. Needed to make applications for Catherine Jana Jones applications to DAR, DRT, and other lineal societies.

Zoltan married Rebecca C. Eurek, 21 April 2001, Galveston County, Texas, per Texas Marriage Index, 1966-2002

Notes for Daryl Lance Allison

Information from birth certificate, marriage certificate and self.

Children of Catherine Jana Jones and Daryl Lance Allison were as follows:

70   i   **Kelsey Alexandra**[6] **Allison**, born 1998 in Houston, Harris County, Texas.

71   ii   **Kimberly Rebecca**[6] **Allison**, born 2002 in Houston, Harris County, Texas.

62. **Rodney Dail**[5] **Blackman III** (Robyn Lane[4] Pulleine, John William[3], Percy Ronald Vail[2], William Taffinder[1]), born 1972 in Houston, Harris County, Texas. He married on 3 May 2008 in Dickinson, Texas **Lori Ann Nelson**, born 1972 in Harris County, Texas, USA, daughter of Larry Oliver Nolen and Grace Louise Lind.

Notes for Rodney Dail Blackman III
Information from family records.

Children of Rodney Dail Blackman III and Lori Ann Nelson were as follows:

72   i   **Lila Basil**[6] **Blackman**, born 2009 in Webster, Harris County, Texas.

Index

Margaret Chloe (1917-2006) — 18
Marjory Louise (1922-2010) — 21
Mary (Twigg) — 1
Myrtle Mary (1876-1947) — 4
Patricia Ann (1912-) — 17
Percy Ronald Vail (1880-1976) — 6
Robyn Lane (1948-) — 38
Samuel Taffinder (1878-1945) — 5
Violet Hyacinth (1882-1969) — 7
William (1808-1892) — 1
William Taffinder (1843-1911) — 1

Raines
Mary Jane (1808-1881) — 1

Rittenhouse
Andrew Pulleine (1968-) — 58
David Laughton (1966-) — 57
Ellis Brooks Jr (1940-) — 35
Ellis Brooks Sr (1912-1978) — 18
Katherine Jane (Laughton) (1941-) — 35
Margaret Chloe (Pulleine) (1917-2006) — 18
Susan Pulleine (1941-) — 36

Shaw
Neoma (1925-) — 29

Smith
Constance Sue (1945-) — 39

Snipes
Sarah Ellen (1914-) — 22

Stark
Virginia Lou — 28

www.ingramcontent.com/pod-product-compliance
Lightning Source LLC
Chambersburg PA
CBHW051450280526
45785CB00003B/1499